Ave Maria

See, Learn, and Meditate on the

Mysteries of the Rosary

PAULIST PRESS
New York / Mahwah, NJ

Photo credits appear on p. 106.

Originally published as Ave Maria: Vedere, conoscere e meditare I misteri del Rosario
© Copyright 2013 by LIBRERIA EDITRICE VATICANA
00120 Vatican City
www.libreriaeditricevaticana.va

English translation by Sean O'Neill
Copyright © 2015 by Paulist Press

Library of Congress Cataloging-in-Publication Data
Poggio, Maria Rosa.
    [Ave Maria. English]
    Ave Maria : see, learn, and meditate on the mysteries of the rosary / Maria Rosa Poggio.
        pages cm
    "Originally published as Ave Maria: vedere, conoscere e meditare i misteri del Rosario"—Title page verso.
    ISBN 978-0-8091-4931-5 (pbk. : alk. paper) — ISBN 978-1-58768-511-8 (ebook)
    1. Rosary. I. Title.
    BX2163.P5513 2015
    242`.74—dc23
                                                              2015007232

ISBN 978-0-8091-4931-5 (paperback)
ISBN 978-1-58768-511-8 (e-book)

Published by Paulist Press
997 Macarthur Boulevard
Mahwah, New Jersey 07430

www.paulistpress.com

Printed and bound in the
United States of America

See, Know, and Meditate on the
Mysteries of the Rosary

Seeing

The mysteries of revelation and of salvation proclaimed by Christianity throughout universal history give life to each successive day and come to fruition beyond history, in the timelessness of God. From the annunciation to the Virgin in the hidden lowliness of Nazareth to the glory of the resurrection of Christ, from the dark agony of the cross to the bright joy of the assumption of Mary, the mysteries of the Rosary—joyful, sorrowful, glorious, and luminous—tell the story of salvation, above all, through simple but powerful images.

For centuries, the Christian tradition of both East and West has been committed to portraying the good news, the gospel of revelation and salvation, in visible images of the invisible mystery of God that is embodied in history, is revealed, and saves.

And so it is with the images of the mysteries of the Rosary that the journey of emotion, study, and prayer begins, for from that moving vision we can pass to the knowledge of the fundamental contents of faith and then say the prayers—first with the head, then with the heart, and then with words—that the tradition of the centuries has given us, and that the Church, our Mother and Teacher, even today invites us to recite.

Knowing

The twenty mysteries of the Rosary are a kind of synthesis of the fundamental contents of the Christian faith. Retracing these mysteries is like reviewing the truths of the Creed and venturing into a kind of grand synthesis of the Catechism. Precisely for this reason, it is desirable to, as it were, "round off" the commentary on the content of each stage of the Rosary with a quote from the *Catechism of the Catholic Church*, especially to emphasize their importance—and, in some ways, even to enter into dialogue with them!

Meditating

Seeing and learning about the mysteries of the Rosary is not an end in itself, but is actually a powerful call to prayer: primarily to support meditation and personal prayer, but also to build a useful toolkit and aid for those who are regularly called to lead communal prayer using the Rosary itself.

Contents

How to Recite the Rosary

In the name of the Father, and of the Son, and of the Holy Spirit.
Oh God come to my assistance.
Lord, make haste to help me.
Glory be to the Father, and to the Son, and to the Holy Spirit.
As it was in the beginning, is now, and ever shall be,
world without end.
Amen.

At every decade, the "mystery" is announced, for example, the first mystery: "the Annunciation."

After a brief pause for reflection, recite one **Our Father**, ten **Hail Marys**, and a **Glory Be**.

At each decade, an invocation can be added.

At the end of the Rosary, the Litany of Loreto or other Marian prayers can be recited.

Our Father, Who art in Heaven, hallowed be Thy name; Thy Kingdom come, Thy will be done on earth as it is in Heaven. Give us this day our daily bread; and forgive us our trespasses as we forgive those who trespass against us; and lead us not into temptation, but deliver us from evil. Amen.

Hail Mary, full of grace. The Lord is with thee. Blessed art thou among women, and blessed is the fruit of thy womb, Jesus. Holy Mary, Mother of God, pray for us sinners, now and at the hour of our death. Amen.

Glory Be to the Father, and to the Son, and to the Holy Spirit. As it was in the beginning, is now, and ever shall be, world without end. Amen.

The Joyful Mysteries

Giovanni di Paolo, *The Annunciation* (with heraldic symbols), 1445, Vatican City, Vatican Apostolic Palaces, Vatican Museums, Room II.

Antonello da Messina, *Annunciation*, 1476, oil on panel, 45 x 34.5 cm, Palermo, Abatellis Palace Regional Gallery.

1. *The Annunciation*

The picture here is a work by Antonello da Messina (1430–79), a small oil panel that is stored at the Abatellis Palace at Palermo. In the painting, the artist interprets the theme of the annunciation in a unique way. According to commentators, Antonello painted Mary just at the moment when she accepts God's plan, or when Gabriel has just left and everything has already happened.

Our attention is completely focused on Mary. We can observe how the details of the perfect oval of the face of the Virgin have been realized, and how the artist intends to depict for us the figure of a simple young woman of Galilee. Mary's quiet, ecstatic, and regal gaze is focused on the lower left corner, from which light is shining where the angel is most likely to be.

The artist manages to render the emotions and attitudes of Mary through the details of the hands. Her right hand is raised in a gesture that can be interpreted either as an expression of fear about what is happening to her, or as the moment when Mary accepts God's plan. This gesture of the hand and her calm and serene gaze speak of Mary's yes to the angel.

Mary's left hand is trying to gather in her veil as a sign of modesty and chastity. Mary responds to the angel, who announces that she will become the Mother of God, that she does not know how all this can come about because she has not known a man. Her figure is simple and basic, wrapped in a simple blue veil that covers the upper part of her body. The figure of Mary emerges from the darkness of the background, and around her the light from God shines, testifying to his presence.

At the moment of the annunciation, Mary is reading from the Book of Hours, or from the Scriptures, which is still lying open in front of her and placed on the lectern. One page of the book is raised, almost as though a light puff of wind, or perhaps the wind of the Spirit, had just lifted it.

The angel Gabriel was sent by God to a town in Galilee called Nazareth, to a virgin engaged to a man whose name was Joseph, of the house of David. The virgin's name was Mary. And he came to her and said, "Greetings, favored one! The Lord is with you." But she was much perplexed by his words and pondered what sort of greeting this might be. The angel said to her, "Do not be afraid, Mary, for you have found favor with God. And now, you will conceive in your womb and bear a son, and you will name him Jesus. He will be great, and will be called the Son of the Most High, and the Lord God will give to him the throne of his ancestor David. He will reign over the house of Jacob forever, and of his kingdom there will be no end." Mary said to the angel, "How can this be, since I am a virgin?" The angel said to her, "The Holy Spirit will come upon you, and the power of the Most High will overshadow you; therefore the child to be born will be holy; he will be called Son of God. And now, your relative Elizabeth in her old age has also conceived a son; and this is the sixth month for her who was said to be barren. For nothing will be impossible with God." Then Mary said, "Here am I, the servant of the Lord; let it be with me according to your word." Then the angel departed from her.

Luke 1:26–38

The Announcement to Mary

According to John, an angel appears to Mary and announces the future birth of the Son of God, saying "Rejoice," which can best be rendered as the equivalent of "Greetings" or "Hail." These are truly words of joy because they announce the fulfillment of the messianic promises. Israel was awaiting the messianic era that would usher in the kingdom of God, when YHWH would rule directly over his people. The long-awaited God is finally coming. Mary is hailed as "full of grace," that is, filled with all of the gifts and the favor of God. The words that the angel uses to describe Jesus perfectly illustrate the figure of the Messiah (Isa 9:6; 78:14; 2 Sam 7:1; Dan 7:14).

4

The power of the Most High will cover Mary with its shadow. Here, Luke recalls the image of the shining cloud, a sign of the presence of YHWH which followed the people in the desert, and which was a sign of his strength and power (Exod 13:22; 19:16; 24:16).

Mary is a virgin betrothed to Joseph, and does not understand how the words of the angel can happen. Despite her initial surprise, Mary accepts God's plan and becomes the Mother of Jesus.

The author of the Gospel of Luke was inspired by some of the models in the Old Testament where an angel is sent by God to announce a mission (Judg 6:11–24). It is interesting to read what the Book of Judges tells of the birth of Samson (Judg 13:2–7). A messenger from God, an angel, appears to a woman who is considered barren to announce the birth of a son. Through the conception of a child by a barren woman, the biblical author tells us that the God of the Bible is not far away, but is directly involved in the lives of human beings and able to create the conditions within which salvation history must happen. However, while Samson was born of a barren woman in the context of normal married life with human and sexual relationships, Jesus will be born of a virgin because he is the Son of God.

The Announcement of the Birth of the Messiah Savior

Luke's story is reminiscent of the text in Isaiah 7:10–14: "Again the LORD spoke to Ahaz, saying, Ask a sign of the LORD your God; let it be deep as Sheol or high as heaven. But Ahaz said, I will not ask, and I will not put the LORD to the test. Then Isaiah said: 'Hear then, O house of David! Is it too little for you to weary mortals, that you weary my God also? Therefore the Lord himself will give you a sign. Look, the young woman is with child and shall bear a son, and shall name him Immanuel.'"

In this passage, the English "young woman" translates the Hebrew *almâ*, which indicates a young woman who is not necessarily married. In this case, the *almâ* is the young wife of the king and the sign given by God through the prophet will be the birth of an heir, a sign of the continuation of the dynasty.

The text of Isaiah is related to the royal messianic prophecies that the prophet Nathan had already introduced (2 Sam 7) and that would be taken up and developed later by other prophets (Mic 4:4; Ezek 34:23; Hag 2:23). Israel was waiting for a royal Messiah through whom God would give salvation to his people. Nevertheless, this salvation would only find its fulfillment as long as the line of David did not fail. The Prophet commands that this son of the king be given the name Emmanuel, God with us, following a pattern often found in the Old Testament where God imposes or changes the name of those who have a special role in his plan of salvation. The angel indicates to Mary the name of the Son of God that will be born to her: Jesus. It is Jesus who will be the true Emmanuel, the expected one of Israel, the God who is truly with us.

The scene presented by Isaiah has in it a solemnity that goes far beyond the simple, though dramatic, situation that occurs in Ahaz's experience. Therefore, the evangelists and the whole of Christian tradition have legitimately chosen to apply this prophecy to the descendant of David, who can be regarded as the awaited Messiah, the son of the King, God. The name imposed directly on Jesus reminds us of his messianic function: God saves. Jesus, the Son of God, is the Savior of all men from the moment of his birth.

With the Nicene Creed, we answer by confessing: "For us men and for our salvation he came down from heaven; by the power of the Holy Spirit, he became incarnate of the Virgin Mary, and was made man."

Catechism of the Catholic Church 456

Giovanni di Paolo, *The Annunciation*

This is the way the painter Giovanni di Paolo wanted to indelibly mark the moment when the angel Gabriel appears to Mary to announce the news of the conception of the Son of God.

The artist has rendered the importance of the moment using the richness of gold. Mary was chosen to be the Mother of the Son of God, the Mother of a king, and the rich glow of gold highlights that.

At center stage, we find Gabriel addressing Mary, who is on the right.

Mary is seated on a throne because she is considered Queen and is absorbed in prayer. From above, the hand of God the Father, reaches out to Mary, holding three fingers raised, indicating the Trinity. Between God the Father and Mary we see a small dove, the symbol of the Holy Spirit sent to Mary to bring about in her the incarnation of Jesus. A large vase containing a lily, the sign of purity and virginity, is between Gabriel and Mary.

Gabriel holds an olive branch, symbolizing the Passover of Jesus. This is how the painter wishes to fully show the mystery of Christ, his incarnation recalled in the annunciation to Mary, but also his passion, death, and resurrection, which are shown in the symbol of the olive branch. When we recite the Rosary, the path of our meditation begins with the mystery of the incarnation of the Son of God, the Messiah, who was awaited by Israel. However, we must also keep in mind that in God's plan, the incarnation is carried out for the redemption of all humanity. The mysteries of the incarnation and redemption are tied to each other.

Gabriel points to the dove, the symbol of the Holy Spirit, which is coming down surrounded by seraphim. It will be through the work of the Holy Spirit that Mary will conceive Jesus, the Son of God.

Jacopo Carucci, called Pontormo, *The Visitation*, 1528–30, oil panel, 202 x 156 cm, Rectory of Saints Michael and Francis.

2. The Visitation

Jacopo Carucci, called Pontormo,
The Visitation

This oil panel (1528–30) is housed in the church of St. Michael in Carmignano and is the work of Jacopo Carucci called Pontormo. The artist was inspired by the Gospel of Luke (1:41–42), where the story of Mary's visit to St. Elizabeth is recounted.

Here we see four figures arranged in a square formation. The two women in the background are maids: they are a step behind the two cousins and look directly and fixedly at the viewer, inviting us to reflect and meditate on the scene.

Mary and Elizabeth embrace in a visible relationship of familiarity. The artist intends to highlight the figures of the two women who share a similar destiny. Elizabeth, who was thought to be barren, will give birth to John, while Mary the Virgin, woman of Galilee, will give birth to the Son of God. It is in this embrace of powerful mutual affection that Elizabeth realizes that Mary is pregnant.

The composition is dominated by silence, and the two maids express this with their silent, almost rigid, presence. No other elements or further embellishments are necessary to give importance to this moment. And it is with silence that the maids invite the viewer to join the solemnity of the moment. What emerges from the figures of Mary and Elizabeth is, above all, the condition of motherhood. The eyes of the two women transmit the knowledge of their sons' destinies.

The fluttering robes are puffed out, as though to emphasize the fertility and pregnancy of two women: the effect makes the two mother figures almost resemble flowers, bursting with life.

Elizabeth and Mary are symbols of the Old and the New Testaments. John the Baptist will be the last prophet of the Old Testament. Jesus is the Word of God made flesh, and from his preaching will emerge the New Testament.

In those days Mary set out and went with haste to a Judean town in the hill country, where she entered the house of Zechariah and greeted Elizabeth. When Elizabeth heard Mary's greeting, the child leaped in her womb. And Elizabeth was filled with the Holy Spirit and exclaimed with a loud cry, "Blessed are you among women, and blessed is the fruit of your womb. And why has this happened to me, that the mother of my Lord comes to me? For as soon as I heard the sound of your greeting, the child in my womb leaped for joy. And blessed is she who believed that there would be a fulfillment of what was spoken to her by the Lord."

Luke 1:39–45

Mary's Concern for Elizabeth

In chapters 1–2 of his Gospel, Luke the Evangelist lays out the births of John the Baptist and Jesus like a diptych. Luke presents the events from Mary's point of view, while Matthew presents them from Joseph's (Matt 1:18–25).

Elizabeth was the wife of the priest Zechariah. Throughout their marriage, although they were righteous before God, the couple did not have any children. One day, while offering the incense in the temple, Zechariah received the announcement from an angel reassuring him that God had answered his prayers: his wife would finally have a son whom he must name John.

This passage presents Mary, who has traveled to see her cousin. The two women meet and stand facing each other: Elizabeth, although she was barren, is expecting a baby and will soon give birth; Mary, despite being a virgin, is with child through the Holy Spirit.

Elizabeth's Blessing

Elizabeth realizes by the movements of the child in her womb, which every mother learns to understand and read, that her longed-for son is agitated, almost as if acknowledging that the baby in Mary's womb is the awaited Messiah. Elizabeth is believed to be at that time especially favored by God who allows her to experience this encounter with the Lord, and the gift of the Holy Spirit ensures that she can welcome Mary, who goes far beyond the normal prescription of courtesy. Elizabeth proclaims Mary to be blessed among all women since she is bearing the blessed fruit of her womb. Mary is blessed by God in a special way because she is the Mother of the Lord. The blessedness of Mary is a consequence of her faith, her commitment to God's plan, and the fact that she has agreed to be the Mother of God.

"There was a man sent from God, whose name was John." John was "filled with the Holy Spirit even from his mother's womb" by Christ himself, whom the Virgin Mary had just conceived by the Holy Spirit. Mary's visitation to Elizabeth thus became a visit from God to his people.

Catechism of the Catholic Church 717

11

3. The Nativity

This work is by Sano di Pietro (1406–81) and dates back to about 1445. It is preserved in the Vatican Museums in Rome.

Over the centuries, the Church has had to adjust the criterion by which the nativity of Jesus is depicted in order to eliminate or amend those iconographies that could give rise to misunderstandings regarding the faith. The oldest representations show Mary lying on her side and the baby having just been born. But this iconography, in which the human labor of childbirth is depicted, allowed only one aspect of the mystery to be emphasized, that of the birth of Jesus the man, even if the artist had no intention of falling into heresy or causing christological misunderstandings. Thereafter, reproductions of the nativity of Jesus always depict the Madonna with the child in her arms or already laid in the manger, to emphasize her divine motherhood. Sano di Pietro is part of this iconographic tradition. Jesus has just been born and is laid on some straw or hay, which was to serve as food for the donkey and the ox. The young mother has just given birth, but the artist presents her kneeling in prayer and adoration before her Son. The labor pains of the virgin birth have left no traces upon her, and because of this, she seems not to have suffered physically. On the right, an aged Joseph is astonished by what has occurred. The Holy Family gathers under a portico, an image that closely resembles that used by Giotto.

Just above Jesus appears the dove, the symbol for the Holy Spirit. Higher still we see that the sky almost comes down to meet the earth, for in him heaven and earth would meet. Behind the manger are the ox and the donkey, neither of which is mentioned in either the Gospel of Luke, nor in Matthew's, but rather in the Apocryphal Gospels. The donkey can be regarded as a metaphor to represent the pagans, while the ox represents the people who are subject to the yoke of the Mosaic Law, namely the Jews. Nevertheless, Jesus became man to save all humanity, including both the converts who came from paganism and the children of Israel.

Sano di Pietro, *Nativity and the Annunciation to the Shepherds*, ca. 1445, section of the predella, painted on wood, 31.5 x 45 cm, Vatican City, Vatican Apostolic Palace, Vatican Museums, Room II.

In those days a decree went out from Emperor Augustus that all the world should be registered. This was the first registration and was taken while Quirinius was governor of Syria. All went to their own towns to be registered. Joseph also went from the town of Nazareth in Galilee to Judea, to the city of David called Bethlehem, because he was descended from the house and family of David. He went to be registered with Mary, to whom he was engaged and who was expecting a child. While they were there, the time came for her to deliver her child. And she gave birth to her firstborn son and wrapped him in bands of cloth, and laid him in a manger, because there was no place for them in the inn.

In that region there were shepherds living in the fields, keeping watch over their flock by night. Then an angel of the Lord stood before them, and the glory of the Lord shone around them, and they were terrified. But the angel said to them, "Do not be afraid; for see—I am bringing you good news of great joy for all the people: to you is born this day in the city of David a Savior, who is the Messiah, the Lord. This will be a sign for you: you will find a child wrapped in bands of cloth and lying in a manger." And suddenly there was with the angel a multitude of the heavenly host, praising God and saying, "Glory to God in the highest heaven, and on earth peace among those whom he favors!" When the angels had left them and gone into heaven, the shepherds said to one another, "Let us go now to Bethlehem and see this thing that has taken place, which the Lord has made known to us." So they went with haste and found Mary and Joseph, and the child lying in the manger. When they saw this, they made known what had been told them about this child; and all who heard it were amazed at what the shepherds told them. But Mary treasured all these words and pondered them in her heart. The shepherds returned, glorifying and praising God for all they had heard and seen, as it had been told them.

Luke 2:1–20

Jesus, the Firstborn

The Roman Empire used to make a census of the population with the purpose of updating the records of those who would have to pay taxes. However, we are not aware of any census of the whole empire made under Caesar Augustus; the previous passage is our only source. Most likely Luke has extended to the Empire a local event that occurred when Quirinius was legate of Syria. Jesus was born in Bethlehem in Judea to Mary of Nazareth, wife of Joseph of the family of David. The royal Messiah awaited by Israel would have to be descended from David. Mary has already been welcomed by Joseph into his home, and has become his wife. This is why she accompanies her husband.

The couple is in Bethlehem to register with the census in compliance with the decree of Caesar Augustus, but Mary is at the end of her pregnancy and gives birth to her firstborn son (*prototokos*). The text does not use *monogenês*, only-begotten son.

Luke knows Greek well, and he uses the language appropriately: by using the term *prototokos*, the evangelist intends to emphasize that Jesus is the firstborn (*bekor* in Hebrew) because according to the Law, eldest sons were to be consecrated to God and were his property (Ezek 13:2), and had to be redeemed with a sacrifice. Therefore, the word used does not imply that after this firstborn other children were born to Mary and Joseph.

No Room at the *Katalyma*...

At the time of Jesus, the houses were often dug into the ground. The innermost part was intended for animals. So that the animals could feed, a manger was placed at the bottom. Just outside, often placed in a raised area, was the *katalyma*: this was the part of the house where members of a Jewish family lived.

Joseph and Mary had gone to Bethlehem and were hosted by their relatives, but there was not room for everyone in the *katalyma*, that is, in the part of the house normally used by the family, so they had to be accommodated in the part reserved for the animals. After Jesus was born, he was placed in the manger.

...A Savior Is Born for Us

The text speaks of the presence of an angel (*anghelos*), a messenger, one who brings good news. The announcement brought by this divine messenger is truly stirring news that has to do with salvation: "A savior is born for you, who is Christ the Lord." The words used in this sentence identify Jesus as the Messiah (Hebrew *Mašía*, translated by the Greek word *Christòs*, anointed one), the one who is awaited by Israel; the Savior (in Greek *Sôter*, one who saves); and as Lord by the Greek word *Kurios*, which translates the Hebrew *Adonai*, used in the Old Testament to indicate the name of God, YHWH, which it was forbidden to utter. It is therefore not merely the announcement of the birth of a child.

The angel is the herald of God, the true King of Israel, and he announces the birth of his Son, his only heir. This birth is not insignificant for human beings, but calls them to participate in the life of a new era that is beginning at that precise moment. The title of *sôter* was given to emperors, kings, and gods, indicating recognition of help given to those in need. The *sôteria* of Jesus, nevertheless, must be linked to the concept of salvation in the Old Testament (Isa 44:6; 45:15, 21; Hab 3:18; Ps 79[78]:9). It is an interior and spiritual salvation. Jesus would have to struggle all his life against the material conception of salvation and messiahship by which others sought to limit his influence to the purely political, in order to affirm the spiritual dimension of his mission.

The Peace of the Messiah

God loves us, is near to us, and because of this we are called to enter into his peace. The Hebrew shalom did not simply consist of the absence of war, but came to mean a peace that also extended into the life of the people. The realization of peace would be made manifest when, in the

16

presence of the Messiah, humanity would no longer need anything. Now that moment had come: God loves us and shows us this love through the incarnation of his Son. Angels and human beings are united in giving glory to God. The theme of the glorification of God is dear to Luke and he speaks of it and highlights it often in his Gospel (1:64; 2:28, 38; 5:25–26; 7:16; 13:13; 17:15, 18; 18:43; 19:37; 23:47; 24:53).

The Shepherds

The first to receive the news of the birth of the Son of God are the shepherds. In the Old Testament, the figure of the shepherd symbolized God's approval of someone. Abel and David were shepherds; Abraham had many flocks and so did the patriarchs. This can certainly be interpreted as a sign of the pastoral culture that was present in at least a part of Israel. However, God was also the shepherd of his people.

Over time, the figure of the shepherd changed, at least in part. The people of Israel, which in the early days had been nomadic, eventually settled down and, although shepherds were still numerous, they no longer enjoyed such a high reputation. The old struggle between nomads and settlers also manifested itself in this way.

It was arduous for shepherds to observe the laws of ritual purity scrupulously; they also led a simple, frugal life, and they were often accused of carrying out raids at the expense of the peasants. Their testimony in a trial was scorned, and they could not hold the office of judge. God, however, sends his messengers first to the shepherds. In this context, the shepherds play the role reserved in Scripture for the *anawim*, the poor of YHWH of which Luke speaks in the section of the Gospel that presents the Beatitudes. The *anawim*, the poor of YHWH, belonged to the rest of Israel, the part that had always remained faithful to God and had passed unscathed through the many punishments that the people had experienced during the history of salvation. The *anawim*, therefore, represent the best of the people, the part that remained faithful, even though they were humble and despised by all.

The shepherds truly experience a theophany (a manifestation of God), for the glory of the Lord surrounds them, yet they are still alive: God himself communicates with the shepherds. This is something new. The belief of humankind in the Old Testament was that one who saw God lost their life. God is indeed so powerful, and his holiness so strong, that human life cannot withstand his revealed presence.

In Exodus, God says to Moses, "Come no closer! Remove the sandals from your feet, for the place on which you are standing is holy ground" (Exod 3:5). It is therefore understandable that the shepherds (as well as Moses in Exod 3:6b) are struck with great fear. The glory of God encompasses them and yet they are still alive. A great joy is revealed to them, which in the context of the Gospel is an experience located between two dimensions. On the one hand, there is the freedom of God who intervenes in human history, and on the other is the human hope that amounts to a certainty that what was promised by God, the coming of the Messiah, has finally arrived.

The event was attended by a multitude of angels: we are in the presence of the courts of the God of Israel who are gathered for the birth of the heir; in other words, at this very moment everything takes place in God's presence.

A Pivotal Event

The birth of Jesus is an event of crucial importance: this event radiates with the glory and praise that rise from humankind to God; salvation, joy, and peace come to humanity from God, and these elements are inherent to the messianic era. The presence of God in human flesh therefore has a salvific value that cannot remain hidden, but should be known by all. And that is what shepherds do: as soon as they receive the announcement of the birth of Jesus, they cannot keep the news to themselves. However, Mary kept these things within her heart. So with these two simple descriptions, Luke shows us two possible paths for all Christians. Faith can be lived out in active mission, but also in prayer and contemplation.

To the shepherds, the angel announced the birth of Jesus as the Messiah promised to Israel: "To you is born this day in the city of David a Savior, who is Christ the Lord" [Luke 2:11]. From the beginning he was "the one whom the Father consecrated and sent into the world" [John 10:36], conceived as "holy" in Mary's virginal womb. God called Joseph to "take Mary as your wife, for that which is conceived in her is of the Holy Spirit" [Matt 1:20], so that Jesus, "who is called Christ" [Matt 1:16], should be born of Joseph's spouse into the messianic lineage of David.

Catechism of the Catholic Church 437

Called in the Gospels "the mother of Jesus" [John 2:1; 19:25], Mary is acclaimed by Elizabeth, at the prompting of the Spirit and even before the birth of her son, as "the mother of my Lord" [Luke 1:43]. In fact, the One whom she conceived as man by the Holy Spirit, who truly became her Son according to the flesh, was none other than the Father's eternal Son, the second person of the Holy Trinity. Hence the Church confesses that Mary is truly "Mother of God."

Catechism of the Catholic Church 495

To become a child in relation to God is the condition for entering the kingdom. For this, we must humble ourselves and become little. Even more: to become "children of God" we must be "born from above" or "born of God" [John 3:7]. Only when Christ is formed in us will the mystery of Christmas be fulfilled in us. Christmas is the mystery of this "marvelous exchange."

Catechism of the Catholic Church 526

Raphael Sanzio, *Presentation of Jesus in the Temple*, 1502–4, section of the predella, oil tempera on panel, 39 x 190 cm, Vatican City, Vatican Museums, Room VIII.

4. The Presentation

Raphael Sanzio,
Presentation of Jesus in the Temple

Raphael Sanzio, who was born in Urbino in 1483 and died in Rome in 1520, executed the Oddi Altarpiece, an oil tempera painting on panel, now kept in the Vatican Museums in Rome.

The scene of the Presentation of Jesus in the temple is located in the predella and records three moments of the life of Jesus:

–The annunciation

–The adoration of the Magi

–The presentation in the temple

In painting this work, Raphael was inspired by the Fano Altarpiece. He wanted to portray the episode in a great variety of colors.

The scene takes place in the temple of Jerusalem, which is rendered using the canons of Renaissance architecture.

Two columns define the space within which the artist has placed the main characters. In the foreground we see:

–Mary holding Jesus in her arms;

–The high priest;

–An aged Joseph who is holding out his left hand toward the child.

Notice how Jesus turns toward his Mother and not toward Joseph.

Behind these characters, the door of the Holy of Holies lies open, and it seems like a dark cave, because the light is falling on the Lord who is placed before our eyes as a tiny, eight-day-old baby.

When the time came for their purification according to the law of Moses, they brought him up to Jerusalem to present him to the Lord (as it is written in the law of the Lord, "Every firstborn male shall be designated as holy to the Lord"), and they offered a sacrifice according to what is stated in the law of the Lord, "a pair of turtledoves or two young pigeons."

Now there was a man in Jerusalem whose name was Simeon; this man was righteous and devout, looking forward to the consolation of Israel, and the Holy Spirit rested on him. It had been revealed to him by the Holy Spirit that he would not see death before he had seen the Lord's Messiah. Guided by the Spirit, Simeon came into the temple; and when the parents brought in the child Jesus, to do for him what was customary under the law, Simeon took him in his arms and praised God, saying, "Master, now you are dismissing your servant in peace, according to your word; for my eyes have seen your salvation, which you have prepared in the presence of all peoples, a light for revelation to the Gentiles and for glory to your people Israel." And the child's father and mother were amazed at what was being said about him. Then Simeon blessed them and said to his mother Mary, "This child is destined for the falling and the rising of many in Israel, and to be a sign that will be opposed so that the inner thoughts of many will be revealed—and a sword will pierce your own soul too." There was also a prophet, Anna the daughter of Phanuel, of the tribe of Asher. She was of a great age, having lived with her husband seven years after her marriage, then as a widow to the age of eighty-four. She never left the temple but worshiped there with fasting and prayer night and day. At that moment she came, and began to praise God and to speak about the child to all who were looking for the redemption of Jerusalem.

Luke 2:22–38

Mary and Joseph, Observant Jews

Luke emphasizes, as he did for the parents of John the Baptist, that Mary and Joseph fulfill all ritual acts prescribed by the Law, which required the mother to purify herself after giving birth (she was deemed to be unclean for seven days; see Lev 12:2–8), while the firstborn son had to be consecrated to God. It was not mandatory that the child be presented at the temple, but for the evangelist this event foreshadows the passion, death, and resurrection of Jesus. It is interesting that one interpretation says that by presenting Jesus in the temple, Mary, who was of the priestly family, is carrying out a purification for the sons of Levi by bringing God an offering that is truly pleasing to him (Mal 3:1–4), that is, Jesus himself.

In order to redeem the firstborn, the parents had to offer a sum of money. The parents of Jesus bring the offering of the poor, two turtledoves, or two young pigeons. However, Jesus is the Holy One because he is God. The Mother, Mary, has been overshadowed by the glory of God who resides in the temple. That is why she has become Jesus' Mother and is therefore pure, just as Jesus is pure and has no need to be rededicated.

Jesus is presented to the Lord. According to Luke, Jesus has the role of priest, he is the Messiah priest capable of offering a sacrifice that is valid, pure, acceptable to the Lord, and different from the purely external sacrifices with which God was so displeased.

But here Jesus is also presented as the victim offered to God.

Simeon and Anna

Then two other characters arrive on the scene: Simeon and Anna.

Simeon is described as a righteous and devout man, looking forward "to the consolation of Israel," the event that, as the prophets foretold, would bring salvation.

Luke wants the reader to realize that this moment is important, and so he mentions the Holy Spirit three times. When Simeon sees the baby, he understands that he has seen the Messiah. Simeon's sight is affected by the Spirit so that he can see clearly, and in the Nunc Dimittis we have an outpouring of the Spirit. Simeon takes Jesus in his arms, blesses God, and takes on the priestly role by presenting the offering and at the same time pronouncing the blessing. In addition, Simeon also blesses the parents and utters a prophecy over the child, indicating his purpose, his mission, and his destiny. In this hymn, which is probably a reworking by the same Luke who used material from Isaiah, Simeon expresses his joy for all that God had said, all he had promised has come true: his lifetime of waiting and hoping was not in vain. Jesus is the bearer of salvation for all peoples, for all who wish to receive it, and it therefore has a universal significance that goes far beyond that envisaged by Israel as only valid for those who belonged to the Jewish people. Jesus will be the light that illuminates all the nations of the earth (the peoples), those who believe in him, but he will also be the glory of Israel, because the salvation for the whole universe will come from the Jewish people itself.

However, there will be no consensus about Jesus. Jesus will be a sign of contradiction: people will be divided over him. There will be people who accept him as the Son of God, but there will also be those who, when faced with these words, will be scandalized because God, who is pure spirit, the God who is unique, cannot have children. Those who reject him will fall and through their choice become guilty.

Here Luke uses the symbol of the sword, which can refer to Ezekiel 14:17 or to Zechariah 12:10. However, we must remember that the sword can be used not only as a weapon to kill or injure, but also to divide, and thus also to discriminate. It is precisely because of this that those who believe in Jesus can be saved.

Here Mary does not only represent herself. It is true that a sword will pierce her heart beneath the cross. But Luke is more refined than that. Mary represents Israel, which is often described using the metaphor of a woman. Luke presents Mary as the full realization of this woman of whom the prophets spoke, the daughter of Zion—in reality, Israel.

It is thanks to the fruit of Mary's motherhood that a sword will pass through the people and divide it between those who accept belief in Jesus and those who will be offended by him. The Prophet Isaiah (Isa 49:2) presents us with another image that can be of help. The mouth of the servant of YHWH, through God's intervention, has become a sharp sword, and the Book of Revelation presents us with a horseman from whose mouth comes a sharp sword and who is called "the Word of God." If at this point we combine these two pieces of information, we perceive that the sword that will create this division in Israel is the Word of God, which will show salvation to the people of Israel. So while the Word of God will bring light to all nations, Israel will be divided between those who accept and those who reject Jesus. Because the sense of this image is one of discrimination, this sword also has the meaning of judgment.

According to Judges 4:4 (and 2 Kgs 22:14), there were prophetesses who had a special gift from the Holy Spirit. After a brief marriage, Anna had found herself widowed and dedicated her life to prayer. The prophetess, after seeing the child, speaks of Jesus to all who were waiting for "the redemption of Jerusalem," which would come about only with the coming of the Messiah, whom the prophetess has now seen with her own eyes. So, just as with the shepherds, Anna cannot help but be a messenger of the salvation that was made flesh.

The presentation of Jesus in the temple shows him to be the firstborn Son who belongs to the Lord. With Simeon and Anna, all Israel awaits its encounter with the Savior—the name given to this event in the Byzantine tradition. Jesus is recognized as the long-expected Messiah, the "light to the nations" and the "glory of Israel," but also "a sign that is spoken against." The sword of sorrow predicted for Mary announces Christ's perfect and unique oblation on the cross that will impart the salvation God had "prepared in the presence of all peoples."

Catechism of the Catholic Church 529

Albrecht Dürer, *Jesus among the Teachers*, 1506, oil panel, 64.3 x 80.3 cm, Madrid, Thyssen-Bornemisza Museum.

5. The Finding of Jesus in the Temple

> Albrecht Dürer,
> **Jesus among the Teachers**

This painting is a panel of poplar wood painted in oil, displayed at the Thyssen-Bornemisza Museum in Madrid, and is the work of Albrecht Dürer. The work was carried out by the artist employing a new technique; he began by using a cast of characters who occupy the entire space and seems to loom over the young Jesus at the center of the scene. The artist has succeeded in representing the six teachers as if they were not anchored to the ground, because they almost seem to float in the air. Just like their bodies, even their religious musings cannot find a valid basis, while Jesus remains quite solid in his central position. The voice of Jesus and of the teachers is transferred to their gestures. So the hands of one of the teachers seem to want to touch those of Jesus to silence him. Meanwhile, Jesus is simply listing on his fingers the arguments in favor of his thesis. However, Jesus has an absent look and seems almost sad.

If the face of Jesus appears transfigured by the humanity of his emotions, the faces of the teachers have passed into envy, malice, and feelings that make them look more like animals than men who are devoted to the inner search and to spirituality.

Their culture and the certainties of these scholars are based on what they have had to study hard throughout their lives: the large open volumes are meant to signify accumulated knowledge that did not help them to progress toward wisdom, but turned them into arrogant old men who are earnestly striving to get the better of Jesus by repeating their own tired teachings.

Now every year his parents went to Jerusalem for the festival of the Passover. And when he was twelve years old, they went up as usual for the festival. When the festival was ended and they started to return, the boy Jesus stayed behind in Jerusalem, but his parents did not know it. Assuming that he was in the group of travelers, they went a day's journey. Then they started to look for him among their relatives and friends. When they did not find him, they returned to Jerusalem to search for him. After three days they found him in the temple, sitting among the teachers, listening to them and asking them questions. And all who heard him were amazed at his understanding and his answers. When his parents saw him they were astonished; and his mother said to him, "Child, why have you treated us like this? Look, your father and I have been searching for you in great anxiety." He said to them, "Why were you searching for me? Did you not know that I must be in my Father's house?" But they did not understand what he said to them. Then he went down with them and came to Nazareth, and was obedient to them. His mother treasured all these things in her heart. And Jesus increased in wisdom and in years, and in divine and human favor.

Luke 2:41–52

In Jerusalem for the Passover

Since he is twelve years old and therefore an adult under the Law, Jesus is subject to all the religious obligations. The Jews had to travel to Jerusalem at Passover, the Festival of Weeks, and during the Feast of Tabernacles. In the temple, Jesus is engaged in discussion with the doctors of the Law (Luke 2:41–52) and the author brings out the particular wisdom and acuity of both his questions and his answers. Jesus speaks with authority and interprets the Law like an exegete, commenting on the Scriptures correctly. Using this broad-brush approach, Luke wishes to show the quality of the wisdom Jesus had as he grew up. He is not just any man but is the Revealer. His knowledge does not come from the study of Sacred Scripture, but from being the Son of God.

His parents were distraught because they believed Jesus was lost. Jesus answers them that he had to concern himself with the things of his Father's house, but Mary and Joseph did not understand. The lack of understanding is one of Luke's favorite themes (see Luke 9:45; 18:34; 24:25). Hidden behind this lack of understanding, throughout his Gospel, is the mystery of Jesus' passion, for this truth can and should be understood only in the light of the resurrection at Easter.

Eventually, his parents find him, but first they have to spend three days consumed with anguish because of his absence. These three days make us think of the absence of Jesus from his loved ones when he is hidden in the tomb, the fear that racked all his disciples and the experience of the women who received the angels' words: "Why do you look for the living among the dead?" (Luke 24:5b). Here, Luke anticipates what will happen to Jesus: his death, his burial, the three days during which he will be hidden in the darkness of death, only to return resurrected among his people. Jesus became flesh in order to take care of the things of the Father; his mission is focused on that moment.

The expression that Jesus uses, "my Father," indicates not only a special relationship of intimacy and trust between Jesus and God, but also his self-awareness of being the Son of God. However, Mary and Joseph do not understand: even though they are close to Jesus in a special way, he has a greatness that is beyond human comprehension. Mary, who has a special relationship with Jesus, treasures in her heart all that happens almost with an attitude of contemplation. What the mind does not understand can be grasped only with the eyes of faith.

> The finding of Jesus in the temple is the only event that breaks the silence of the Gospels about the hidden years of Jesus. Here Jesus lets us catch a glimpse of the mystery of his total consecration to a mission that flows from his divine sonship: "Did you not know that I must be about my Father's work?" Mary and Joseph did not understand these words, but they accepted them in faith. Mary "kept all these things in her heart" during the years Jesus remained hidden in the silence of an ordinary life.
>
> *Catechism of the Catholic Church* 534

The sorrowful mysteries are centered on the cross of Christ. The cross has been the hallmark of believers in Jesus, crucified and risen, from the earliest years of the Christian community. But the image of the crucified Christ did not catch on right away.

In the first centuries of the Church, the cross appears "empty," as a sign bearing symbolic and salvific significance, but devoid of Christ, who is depicted rather as the Good Shepherd, the Teacher, the Pantocrator, or Lord of All.

During the fifth and sixth centuries, the image of the jeweled cross became popular, a precious symbol of the wealth of the gifts of salvation. Sometimes, as in the apse mosaic in the Basilica of Sant'Apollinare Nuovo in Ravenna, the face of Christ appears, solemn and triumphant, at the center of the composition.

Little by little, during the sixth and seventh centuries, the image of the crucified Christ began to appear on the cross. Since then, the crucifix in various forms—suffering and tortured, or serene and triumphant—has established itself as the icon of Christianity, in all its various experiences and expressions.

All the great artists of history have been confronted with this image, even the most troubled, even nonbelievers.

The work of Graham Sutherland, reproduced here, is an eloquent example of these challenges and of this interpretative power.

In this picture, as in many others by contemporary artists, the theme that dominates is that of humanity suffering, oppressed and crushed by violence, by oppression, by the negative face of power.

Humanity invokes redemption and salvation, but only Christ, crucified and risen, can guarantee them.

The Sorrowful Mysteries

Graham Sutherland, *Study for Crucifixion*, 1947, Vatican City, Vatican Apostolic Palace, Collection of Religious Modern Art.

Giovanni di Paolo, *Prayer of Christ in the Garden of Gethsemane*, the Vatican Museums, predella with episodes from the Passion of Christ, 1430–40, painting on wood panel, 31.5 x 32 cm, Vatican City, Vatican Apostolic Palace, Vatican Picture Gallery, Room II.

1. The Agony in the Garden

Giovanni di Paolo, *Prayer of Christ in the Garden of Gethsemane*

The painting shown here is the work of Giovanni di Paolo, who was born in Siena probably toward the end of the fourteenth century and died there in 1482. This work, which was executed between 1430 and 1435, is housed in the Picture Gallery of the Vatican Museums in Rome. Jesus is facing the biggest personal crisis that a man can experience. He has just finished conducting the final battle against a false image of the Messiah, and the temptations he had to overcome in the desert have returned. This time Jesus is not in a desert. In fact, behind the figures you see lush trees. An angel has taken the place of the tempter: we see the angel on the right in the act of offering Jesus a golden chalice with which he proposes to the Son of God his mission, and the Father's plan.

Jesus is depicted kneeling: he is praying, even though people from that time prayed in a standing position and in some cases prostrated themselves on the ground. Jesus raises his hands toward the cup as a sign of acceptance that his hour has come. The cup reminds all of us that the death of Jesus has the characteristics of sacrifice, the same sacrifice celebrated in the Eucharist.

To the left are Peter, James, and John, asleep after the large Passover meal. They are not far away from Jesus, but it is their oblivious sleep that separates them from him. The three apostles are the same ones that had shared the glory of Jesus' transfiguration, but this time they are unable to stay awake and spiritually vigilant. In the background appear the soldiers who are coming to arrest Jesus; behind them, the city of Jerusalem. The golden sparkling light shines from the halos of the three apostles, of Jesus, of the angel, and of the cup, and elevates these details into the dimension of the divine. The fruits on the trees are also picked out by the light. But what darkness swallows up the garrison of soldiers and the city of Jerusalem! Above, it seems that the sky wants to unleash the events that will occur in a few hours in the city of Zion.

H e came out and went, as was his custom, to the Mount of Olives; and the disciples followed him. When he reached the place, he said to them, "Pray that you may not come into the time of trial." Then he withdrew from them about a stone's throw, knelt down, and prayed, "Father, if you are willing, remove this cup from me; yet, not my will but yours be done." Then an angel from heaven appeared to him and gave him strength. In his anguish he prayed more earnestly, and his sweat became like great drops of blood falling down on the ground. When he got up from prayer, he came to the disciples and found them sleeping because of grief, and he said to them, "Why are you sleeping? Get up and pray that you may not come into the time of trial."

Luke 22:39–46

Jesus Combats Temptation

In the garden on the Mount of Olives (Gethsemane), Jesus invites the apostles to pray and watch so they do not come into the time of trial or temptation. This is one of the most difficult moments in the human experience of Jesus, because it is where the total adherence of Jesus to the plan of his Father is tested. The Jews were waiting for a strong and powerful Messiah who was able to conquer the Romans and establish a kingdom as large and powerful as that of David. Instead, in order to be the Messiah, Jesus must accept death. After his baptism, Jesus had spent time in the desert fasting (forty days for the forty years Israel spent in the desert). During that time, Jesus was tempted by the devil. The enticements used by the devil are those with which every human being has to contend: loving something or someone more than God, loving God only partially, not loving God with all one's might. These three temptations correspond to the proof of compliance with what is prescribed in Deuteronomy 6:5. We must not believe that in order to overcome his time of testing, Jesus did not have to fight to stay true to the Father. In fact, Jesus was tempted in the same way as is every person, but Luke tells us of these moments of trial by placing them at the beginning and at the end of his Gospel, as though they were two parentheses that contain Jesus' whole life. The temptation that Jesus must overcome at this time concerns what kind of Messiah he will be. Is it not possible to find another way? Can he not be the strong and powerful Messiah that Israel was waiting for? Is it possible to avoid suffering and death and to win by power and might? Here the temptation is very strong: Jesus is facing suffering and the darkness of death.

The Terrible Fear of Death

In the face of death, a human being naturally experiences terror, and Jesus even sweats blood. But he resolves to say yes to the Father, to do his will, even if it means that he will lose his life. Jesus points out to the disciples how to obtain perseverance and faithfulness to God: through prayer.

So the apostles who were asleep because of sadness are encouraged by Jesus to stay awake and pray that they may be vigilant, in order to save themselves. In the battle of life the main difference between those who have faith and those who do not lies in the fact that those who have faith do not feel invincible; they know that what they can do does not depend only on them but on the tangible help that God offers them. The person who does not have faith believes himself to be either a superman who can do all things or a wretched person who is not capable of doing anything. Jesus accepts his mission and remains faithful, but he also prays that God's will may be done. In contrast to Jesus, the disciples do not pray and therefore fall into temptation. Without the strength that comes from prayer the disciples will flee before the guards who come to arrest Jesus and Peter will deny him.

> The cup of the New Covenant, which Jesus anticipated when he offered himself at the Last Supper, is afterwards accepted by him from his Father's hands in his agony in the garden at Gethsemani, making himself "obedient unto death." Jesus prays: "My Father, if it be possible, let this cup pass from me..." Thus he expresses the horror that death represented for his human nature. Like ours, his human nature is destined for eternal life; but unlike ours, it is perfectly exempt from sin, the cause of death. Above all, his human nature has been assumed by the divine person of the "Author of life," the "Living One." By accepting in his human will that the Father's will be done, he accepts his death as redemptive, for "he himself bore our sins in his body on the tree" [1 Pet 2:24].
>
> *Catechism of the Catholic Church* 612

Michelangelo Merisi da Caravaggio, *Flagellation of Christ*, 1607–8, oil on canvas, 286 x 213 cm, Naples, Capodimonte Museum.

2. *The Scourging at the Pillar*

Michelangelo Merisi da Caravaggio,
Flagellation of Christ

This picture is the work of Caravaggio. It is an oil painting on canvas, executed by the artist between 1607 and 1608. Today it resides in the Capodimonte Museum in Naples.

In the center of the painting, we find the column to which Christ is bound. On either side we see the two Roman soldiers who are scourging Jesus with great precision, using all their concentration and dedication for this task. If we follow the precise gestures of the two torturers, our eye automatically goes to the third soldier, who is bent over. This third character, according to scholars, could be the representation of human nature, which, because of sin, can no longer stand upright, but has assumed a posture similar to that of animals who cannot raise their gaze to the sky, but only stare at the ground.

The dark setting, from which emerge details of the human bodies in this scene, fully captures the emotional and spiritual nuances of the moment: the bodies of the characters are illuminated by a shaft of light that places them in the foreground, but makes them appear livid. There is a heartbreaking relationship between the sharp light of the bodies and the darkness, as if to indicate the wounds suffered by Christ in the flesh, but also the laceration to which human nature is subjected because of sin. All this shows a tremendous tension that is not only emotional but also physical, and seems to account for the fatigue of the torturers and the pain of Jesus.

T hen Pilate took Jesus and had him flogged.

John 19:1

Tested by the Whip

Jesus was scourged by Pilate according to the Roman method. The scourging had two purposes: first, to "loosen the tongue" of the accused and, second, to have someone who was completely covered in blood to display to the people.

The Roman scourge, or *flagrum* (flagellum), was a whip made of many cords of leather. At the end of the cords, many metal pellets were tied. As they hit the condemned prisoner, these metal tips bit into the flesh, and tore it away.

There were two Roman torturers and between them they alternated their strokes on the back, arms, and legs of the condemned.

The scourging Jesus underwent was terrible, so terrible that the guards were afraid Jesus would die on the road to the place of execution. Therefore they had Simon of Cyrene carry Jesus' cross for him.

"For as by one man's disobedience many were made sinners, so by one man's obedience many will be made righteous." By his obedience unto death, Jesus accomplished the substitution of the suffering Servant, who "makes himself an offering for sin," when "he bore the sin of many," and who "shall make many to be accounted righteous," for "he shall bear their iniquities." Jesus atoned for our faults and made satisfaction for our sins to the Father.

Catechism of the Catholic Church 615

Michelangelo Merisi da Caravaggio, *The Crowning with Thorns*, 1603, oil on canvas, 127 x 165 cm, Vienna, Kunsthistorisches Museum.

3. The Crowning with Thorns

> Michelangelo Merisi da Caravaggio,
> **The Crowning with Thorns**

This oil painting by Caravaggio was completed in 1603 and is stored at the Kunsthistorisches Museum in Vienna.

The artist wanted to put the figure of Christ in the middle of the painting, flanked by two thugs who are torturing him. In order to ensure that the crown of thorns is lodged perfectly in the flesh of Jesus' skull, the two soldiers hammer it with large sticks.

If you look carefully, you can see that Caravaggio places a bundle of thorns on Jesus that almost completely covers his entire head. Very often, however, artists have used a circular crown of thorns intertwined, in an attempt to imitate the crowns of kings in the West. Jesus' crown was actually a kind of cap that covered his head entirely. So we must think of Jesus' crown of thorns as a kind of crude hat formed of intertwined branches. In the picture, Jesus' head is sagging and his body is covered with a scarlet cloak.

The artist organized the composition by dividing it into large triangles, which are in opposition to each other. The result is a painting that is anything but rigid and gives the viewer the impression of capturing the divisions and oppositions that exist, not only between the soldiers and Jesus, but also between the soldiers themselves.

The area on the left of the picture is occupied by a man wearing black armor: this soldier observes the scene and does not take part directly. But his presence is not an error of judgment in the composition because he represents the people of today who believe they have nothing to do with the death of Christ and stand aloof, believing they are on the side of the just because they do nothing. By simply opting out, they bear the responsibility and the blame. In fact, before Jesus, none of us can opt out: each must take a stand.

Then the soldiers of the governor took Jesus into the governor's headquarters, and they gathered the whole cohort around him. They stripped him and put a scarlet robe on him, and after twisting some thorns into a crown, they put it on his head. They put a reed in his right hand and knelt before him and mocked him, saying, "Hail, King of the Jews!" They spat on him, and took the reed and struck him on the head. After mocking him, they stripped him of the robe and put his own clothes on him. Then they led him away to crucify him.

Matthew 27:27–31

The King's Game

The Praetorium was where the magistrate, or in this case the procurator, had his office. The building housed all administrative, military, and judicial offices. Usually the procurator of Judea lived in Caesarea, on the coast of the Mediterranean Sea, but sometimes, when there was a fear that riots were brewing, the procurator, along with a considerable garrison of soldiers, went to Jerusalem. Commentators and historians do not know the exact location of the Praetorium: Some think that on these occasions the procurator was stationed at Herod's palace. Others believe that it was at the Antonia Fortress, a building that had been erected in a prominent position overlooking the temple, the place where Jewish riots were generally started and that offered the possibility of controlling the movements of the Jews.

Archaeologists have discovered some stone slabs belonging to the pavement, the place located in front of the Praetorium, and it is possible to discern the faint patterns of some games engraved on the stone with which the soldiers of the garrison occupied the time. One of these could be the "king's game," which is similar to one practiced during the Saturnalia. This game consisted of the casting of lots among the condemned convicts for a carnival king whom everyone had to obey during the festive period. Once the days of the feast were over, the death sentence was carried out. Jesus is therefore involved in this game of a mock king and is clothed in the *sagum*, the scarlet robe of the Roman soldiers, which was like the purple that adorned a king. Jesus is forced to wear a crown made out of the thorny branches of a bush that is very common in Palestine and is hailed with a greeting that is intended to mimic the way the Roman emperor would be addressed.

For most of their history, the Israelites have been awaiting the coming of the Messiah King, a savior who would free the people from the oppression of the enemy and whose reign would bring peace and prosperity. Now that this Messiah has come, he has been delivered into the hands of the Romans who make fun of him as king. But Jesus truly is the King even if his lordship is not shown through the strength and power of his armies. Jesus is a king who suffers for his people, he is the Suffering Servant (Isa 42; 49; 50:4–11; 52; 53) and he gives his life for the salvation of all.

Finally, the People of God shares in the royal office of Christ. He exercises his kingship by drawing all men to himself through his death and Resurrection. Christ, King and Lord of the universe, made himself the servant of all, for he came "not to be served but to serve, and to give his life as a ransom for many." For the Christian, "to reign is to serve him," particularly when serving "the poor and the suffering, in whom the Church recognizes the image of her poor and suffering founder." The People of God fulfills its royal dignity by a life in keeping with its vocation to serve with Christ.

Catechism of the Catholic Church 786

4. The Carrying of the Cross

> Marco Palmezzano,
> **Christ Carrying His Cross**

This work was executed by Marco Palmezzano (1480–1539). It is a painted panel from the sixteenth century and is housed in the Picture Gallery of the Vatican Museums in Rome.

The subject was often depicted by this artist, and each time he adds more details. Here the painter wanted to focus his attention on the image of Christ on a black background. Christ carries a heavy cross made of sawn timber.

Jesus takes up his cross, which he carries over one of his shoulders. He seems almost to embrace it, as a sign of his commitment to the plan of salvation for all humanity, which can be achieved through this instrument of death.

The artist has painted the intensity of Jesus' hands with his fingers arranged around the cross.

Jesus is suffering, but he is not desperate; he is almost thoughtful and is absorbed in his own pain.

The observer can understand the pain of Christ by looking at the drops of blood that form small rivulets on his forehead. The blond hair of Christ falls softly on his shoulders.

By portraying Jesus alone and excluding from the scene the Roman soldiers who mocked him, the artist tries to emphasize the loneliness of Christ during his passion.

Marco Palmezzano, *Christ Carrying His Cross*, 1537–39(?), oil on canvas, 54.5 x 43 cm, Vatican City, Vatican Apostolic Palace, Vatican Picture Gallery, Room IV

As they led him away, they seized a man, Simon of Cyrene, who was coming from the country, and they laid the cross on him, and made him carry it behind Jesus. A great number of the people followed him, and among them were women who were beating their breasts and wailing for him. But Jesus turned to them and said, "Daughters of Jerusalem, do not weep for me, but weep for yourselves and for your children. For the days are surely coming when they will say, 'Blessed are the barren, and the wombs that never bore, and the breasts that never nursed.' Then they will begin to say to the mountains, 'Fall on us'; and to the hills, 'Cover us.' For if they do this when the wood is green, what will happen when it is dry?"

Two others also, who were criminals, were led away to be put to death with him.

Luke 23:26–32

The Way of Suffering

After he has been tried and sentenced to death, Jesus takes up his cross.

With great effort, he tackles the ascent to Golgotha, the place of execution. But the cross is too heavy for him, because he is weakened by the flogging. So the soldiers force a man from Cyrene to help Jesus: Simon of Cyrene carries the Nazarene's cross for a stretch and becomes for Luke the example of a true disciple, the one who unites himself to the suffering of Christ and helps him to carry his cross.

Jesus is not alone on his way to the cross. There is a multitude just as there was at the time of his entry into Jerusalem, and there are women who beat their breasts and weep for him.

They have compassion for Jesus and raise a lament for him, but they also recognize that they are responsible and admit their faults by beating their breasts.

When Jesus is dead (v. 48) the multitude will beat their breasts too because they understand the injustice that has been committed.

Jesus does not comfort these women, but utters a prophecy warning of a terrible catastrophe, and in apocalyptic terms describes the fate that awaits sinners, an even more terrible punishment when compared to the painful and ignominious death that is being inflicted on a righteous man.

Jesus is not the only one condemned to death on this day: with him are two others, two criminals.

The cross is the unique sacrifice of Christ, the "one mediator between God and men." But because in his incarnate divine person he has in some way united himself to every man, "the possibility of being made partners, in a way known to God, in the paschal mystery" is offered to all men. He calls his disciples to "take up [their] cross and follow [him]," for "Christ also suffered for [us], leaving [us] an example so that [we] should follow in his steps." In fact Jesus desires to associate with his redeeming sacrifice those who were to be its first beneficiaries. This is achieved supremely in the case of his mother, who was associated more intimately than any other person in the mystery of his redemptive suffering.

Catechism of the Catholic Church 618

Masolino da Panicale, ***Crucifixion***, 1428–31, tempera on wood, 53 x 31.6 cm, Vatican City, Vatican Apostolic Palace, Vatican Picture Gallery, Room III.

5. The Crucifixion

Masolino da Panicale, *Crucifixion*

This work was painted by Masolino da Panicale (1383–ca. 1440) in tempera on wood, probably between 1428 and 1431, and it is housed in the Picture Gallery of the Vatican Museums in Rome.

We can see that Jesus was nailed to a cross that is not very tall, on a small hill that is meant to represent the summit of Golgotha. The body of Jesus displays the colors of death, and his head is bowed after having breathed his last.

On the wood above him has been posted the *Titulus Crucis* on which Pilate has had written the reason why Jesus has been condemned: INRI, that is, *Iesus Nazarenus Rex Iudaeorum*, Jesus of Nazareth, King of the Jews. At the top, an imposing three-stemmed palm tree, similar to a processional cross, bears the symbol of the pelican, the bird that in legend wounds her own side in order to feed her chicks. The wood of the cross, the instrument on which Christ spent his blood, is bursting with life.

On either side of Jesus are his mother Mary and the beloved disciple. The scene is full of glittering gold, which refers to the light of divine majesty.

And when they came to a place called Golgotha (which means Place of a Skull), they offered him wine to drink, mixed with gall; but when he tasted it, he would not drink it. And when they had crucified him, they divided his clothes among themselves by casting lots; then they sat down there and kept watch over him. Over his head they put the charge against him, which read, "This is Jesus, the King of the Jews." Then two bandits were crucified with him, one on his right and one on his left. Those who passed by derided him, shaking their heads and saying, "You who would destroy the temple and build it in three days, save yourself! If you are the Son of God, come down from the cross." In the same way the chief priests also, along with the scribes and elders, were mocking him, saying, "He saved others; he cannot save himself. He is the King of Israel; let him come down from the cross now, and we will believe in him. He trusts in God; let God deliver him now, if he wants to; for he said, 'I am God's Son.'" The bandits who were crucified with him also taunted him in the same way. From noon on, darkness came over the whole land until three in the afternoon. And about three o'clock Jesus cried with a loud voice, "Eli, Eli, lema sabachthani?" that is, "My God, my God, why have you forsaken me?" When some of the bystanders heard it, they said, "This man is calling for Elijah." At once one of them ran and got a sponge, filled it with sour wine, put it on a stick, and gave it to him to drink. But the others said, "Wait, let us see whether Elijah will come to save him."

Then Jesus cried again with a loud voice and breathed his last. At that moment the curtain of the temple was torn in two, from top to bottom. The earth shook, and the rocks were split. The tombs also were opened, and many bodies of the saints who had fallen asleep were raised. After his resurrection they came out of the tombs and entered the holy city and appeared to many. Now when the centurion and those with him, who were keeping watch over Jesus, saw the earthquake and what took place, they were terrified and said, "Truly this man was God's Son!" Many women were also there, looking on from a distance; they had followed Jesus from Galilee and had provided for him. Among them were Mary Magdalene, and Mary the mother of James and Joseph, and the mother of the sons of Zebedee.

Matthew 27:33–56

The Terrible Torture of the Cross

Now at the top of Golgotha, Jesus is stripped and nailed to the cross. The place where executions took place was a small hill outside the walls of Jerusalem, called in Hebrew, *Golgotha*, and in Latin *Calvarius*, that is, "the place of the skull."

The Roman cross came in two parts: the *stipes* (vertical pole), a not very tall post that remained in place, driven into the ground, into which was inserted the *patibulum*, the crossbeam that was replaced for each condemned prisoner.

The condemned man could be fastened to the *patibulum* either with nails driven into the center of the wrist or, more usually, bound with strong cords. A single nail, planted just above the ankles, immobilized the legs of the condemned. The executioners would often slash the prisoner's wrist, thereby severing the nerve that controls the thumb. Cutting this nerve causes extreme pain.

The condemned man usually died of asphyxiation because his body weight was supported only by his outstretched arms. In order to breathe, the condemned would have to draw himself up by his arms. A very painful, sometimes prolonged death occurred as he became exhausted, which led to progressive difficulty in breathing. When the condemned could no longer lift himself, he would die within a few minutes.

In order to lengthen the torment, the Romans would place a block of wood, the *suppedaneum*, under the feet of the offender, so that, by bracing himself with his feet, he could raise himself up to breathe, but this action also rotated the wrists around the nails, thus causing excruciating pain. Sometimes, in order to hasten death, the legs of the crucified were broken.

According to the Gospels, Jesus was crucified at the third hour (between nine o'clock in the morning and noon) and died around three in the afternoon. Jesus was executed in the way that was reserved for the worst of criminals.

Jesus refuses to take the pain-relieving drink—a mixture of wine, myrrh, and gall—that the compassionate women of Jerusalem used to prepare for those condemned to death. Shortly afterward, he would refuse the vinegar offered to him by the Roman soldiers, reminding us of Psalm 69:21.

Similarly, the prophecy in another psalm is fulfilled by the game the Roman soldiers played, casting lots for Jesus' clothes (Ps 22:18). Thus we see the fulfillment of prophecies already present in Scripture, not an independent event, but a completion of history.

Alone, Abandoned by All, and Empty

Just before his death, Jesus felt alone, abandoned, and completely empty. Jesus felt lost and he was afraid. However, even in this difficult time, he once again chose to obey the will of his Father and not to yield to the temptation of those who invited him to come down from the cross.

When Jesus cries out (see Ps 22:2), he is uttering a prayer to God that expresses the sense of abandonment felt by Jesus at the hour of death, the situation shared by all humanity. The experience of Jesus on the cross must therefore be understood in light of this psalm. Similarly to the author of the Psalms, Jesus is assured of future triumph and because of that he abandons himself into the hands of the Father.

Some believed that Jesus was calling on Elijah, who, according to tradition, would come to the rescue of the righteous. However, we must remember the tradition that Elijah, who had been taken away from Elisha by a chariot of fire, continued to dwell in the heavens and would descend again to earth before the coming of the Messiah.

With this cry, Jesus dies and gives up his spirit. Immediately afterward, the veil of the temple, the curtain that separated the outer sanctuary from the Holy of Holies, was torn in two. With the consecration of the temple, the Glory of God, represented by the cloud that had followed the people in the desert, had entered the Holy of Holies. Here the veil is torn from top to bottom, the temple is no longer the house of God, and the ancient worship of Israel is no longer legitimate.

Extraordinary Signs

Apocalyptic events follow the death of Jesus: earthquakes, the rocks that split asunder. This is what always happens when there is a theophany, a manifestation of God. Here the dead, who, according to the Jewish belief, would come to life again at the end of time, are resurrected; this is a sign of the eschatological era that begins with the death of Jesus, but also a sign of faith in the resurrection of the dead.

The centurion and those present are filled with awe at this manifestation of the presence of God. It is these spectators who blurt out an affirmation of the divinity of Jesus, "Truly this man was God's Son," not the disciples who have fled from this event. At his hour of pain and death, Jesus has been abandoned by all who had been close to him; the only ones who remained were the women, whose testimony, according to the Jews, was worth exactly half that of a man.

Jesus' violent death was not the result of chance in an unfortunate coincidence of circumstances, but is part of the mystery of God's plan, as St. Peter explains to the Jews of Jerusalem in his first sermon on Pentecost: "This Jesus [was] delivered up according to the definite plan and foreknowledge of God" [Acts 2:23]. This Biblical language does not mean that those who handed him over were merely passive players in a scenario written in advance by God.

Catechism of the Catholic Church 599

Anastasis

This fresco is in the Chora Church in Istanbul and dates from the twelfth century. At the center, you can see the risen Christ, triumphant over death, in all his glory as the Lord of life. He is surrounded by mountains that appear to want to bow down to his divine majesty, the stars in the firmament surrounding him with splendor, and he is clothed by the light of God and of life. With great force he breaks the bolts that lock the doors of the kingdom of the underworld, and with strength and gentleness frees the righteous who were confined in that prison, starting with Adam and Eve, the mother and father of all the "old" humanity. Christ is the New Man, the firstborn of a new creation, which now surrounds him with jubilant new life. The gates of the underworld are uprooted and lie on the ground, death is defeated and finally dies, while the risen Christ reveals that in him is true life, life that will never die.

The Glorious Mysteries

Pietro Perugino, *San Francesco al Prato Resurrection*, ca. 1499, oil on board, 233 x 165 cm, Vatican City, Vatican Apostolic Palace, Vatican Picture Gallery, the Sistine Hall, Gallery of the Library.

1. *The Resurrection*

This work is an oil panel by Pietro Perugino (1448–1523) and resides in the Picture Gallery of the Vatican Museums in Rome.

Here the artist wanted to represent the moment immediately following the resurrection. On the sides of the tomb of Christ—which does not look like one of the typical Jewish graves that were dug into the clay—we can see the sleeping guards who are completely unaware of what is happening.

Sleep accompanies some of the most important moments in the life of Christ, and this is crucial, not only for him but for the whole of humanity. Only one character in the background, who is brandishing a sword, seems to be amazed at what happened.

Above the tomb, the cover of which appears to have been moved aside, Christ stands triumphant in the luminous joy of the resurrection. Angels on both sides worship him.

By choosing to represent Christ suspended above the tomb and not in the act of leaving it, the artist probably wanted to allude to the ascension. Actually, scholars believe that the artist reused the same drawings to make the image of Christ in the ascension in the altarpiece of the Church of Borgo Sansepolcro.

But on the first day of the week, at early dawn, they came to the tomb, taking the spices that they had prepared. They found the stone rolled away from the tomb, but when they went in, they did not find the body. While they were perplexed about this, suddenly two men in dazzling clothes stood beside them. The women were terrified and bowed their faces to the ground, but the men said to them, "Why do you look for the living among the dead? He is not here, but has risen. Remember how he told you, while he was still in Galilee, that the Son of Man must be handed over to sinners, and be crucified, and on the third day rise again." Then they remembered his words, and returning from the tomb, they told all this to the eleven and to all the rest. Now it was Mary Magdalene, Joanna, Mary the mother of James, and the other women with them who told this to the apostles. But these words seemed to them an idle tale, and they did not believe them. But Peter got up and ran to the tomb; stooping and looking in, he saw the linen cloths by themselves; then he went home, amazed at what had happened.

Luke 24:1–12

The Women: The First Witnesses

On Sunday morning, the women go to complete the burial arrangements and find the door of the tomb open: Jesus' body is gone. This fact is essential for their announcement of the resurrection to be credible. Jesus had been buried in the grave, and now he is gone.

While the women are still standing there in amazement, two mysterious men appear. Their shining robes and their words show them to be messengers (angels) of God. They bring the women the good news (gospel) of the resurrection of Jesus, saying, "Why do you look for the living among the dead? He is not here, but has risen." The angels remind the women that Jesus had predicted his resurrection.

The Women Speak the Truth

The first announcement of the resurrection, then, is given to a group of women, but for the Jews, the testimony of a woman in court was worth half that of a man. The women immediately inform the apostles, who do not believe them. Because of the incredible nature of the women's announcement, the apostles prefer to think that it was a hallucination, only the ravings of women. Yet this is the first true proclamation of the gospel of the resurrection!

Peter, however, goes to check: the door really was open and tomb empty. Peter also sees the sheets that had wrapped Jesus' body and is full of wonder.

From Incredulity to Faith

Wonder but also disbelief dominate this narrative, the same skepticism demonstrated by the disciples on the road to Emmaus. However, in itself the empty tomb could also suggest that the corpse had been removed. An empty tomb does not necessarily lead to faith in Jesus, whose resurrection is not only a historical fact, but also an event that signals a salvific intervention by God. In order to move from the declaration that the tomb is empty to belief that Jesus rose from the dead, an act of God is required. The model for this step toward faith is the experience of the women. They take the announcement to the apostles only after hearing what the angels have said; they remind them of what Jesus had said, and therefore they begin to understand what has happened by recalling Jesus' words. It is therefore in this light that the resurrection must be understood.

And so the apostles are perplexed by the empty tomb. This is perhaps surprising, but it is genuine and important for today's Christians. It tells us that they were not superhuman, but ordinary men who, when faced with an exceptional event like this, initially exhibit doubt. If they come to believe, they do so because God helps them. But what really happened? To better understand let us turn to the Gospel of John.

Early on the first day of the week, while it was still dark, Mary Magdalene came to the tomb and saw that the stone had been removed from the tomb. So she ran and went to Simon Peter and the other disciple, the one whom Jesus loved, and said to them, "They have taken the Lord out of the tomb, and we do not know where they have laid him." Then Peter and the other disciple set out and went toward the tomb. The two were running together, but the other disciple outran Peter and reached the tomb first. He bent down to look in and saw the linen wrappings lying there, but he did not go in. Then Simon Peter came, following him, and went into the tomb. He saw the linen wrappings lying there, and the cloth that had been on Jesus' head, not lying with the linen wrappings but rolled up in a place by itself. Then the other disciple, who reached the tomb first, also went in, and he saw and believed; for as yet they did not understand the scripture, that he must rise from the dead. Then the disciples returned to their homes.

John 20:1–10

A Woman Encounters the Mystery

On the first day of the week (which would become Sunday—for Christians, the Lord's Day), Mary Magdalene went to the tomb. While the Synoptics tell us of the presence of more women, John names only Mary Magdalene, but the others are implied when Mary Magdalene speaks in the plural: "We do not know where they have laid him." She most likely went to the tomb to finish the burial arrangements. According to John (John 19:40–42), Jesus was buried in a hurry because it was the day of preparation and the Sabbath was beginning. If they had completed the burial, contact with the corpse would have made them ritually impure, making it impossible for them to perform the rites prescribed for the Sabbath.

The Open and Empty Tomb, the Discarded Shroud

Luke and John say that Peter went to find out what could have happened to Jesus' body. But John also mentions the presence of the "disciple whom Jesus loved," and it is he who arrives at the tomb first, perhaps because he was younger than Peter ("the other disciple outran Peter"). When they arrive at the tomb, the disciple whom Jesus loved bends down and sees the linens, but deferring to Peter, he does not go in. When Peter arrives, he sees the linen that wrapped the body of Jesus and the cloth that had covered his head rolled up separately; the body of Jesus is gone. From what the eyewitnesses could see, it did not appear that the shroud had been torn from the body and abandoned in a heap, as thieves would have left it. Rather, it seemed that Jesus' body had "vanished" and that the grave clothes had been shed. The detail of the linens probably convinced Peter that something remarkable must have happened: grave robbers would not have left the grave clothes that way.

"Why do you seek the living among the dead? He is not here, but has risen"[Luke 24:5–6]. The first element we encounter in the framework of the Easter events is the empty tomb. In itself it is not a direct proof of Resurrection; the absence of Christ's body from the tomb could be explained otherwise. Nonetheless the empty tomb was still an essential sign for all. Its discovery by the disciples was the first step toward recognizing the very fact of the Resurrection. This was the case, first with the holy women, and then with Peter. The disciple "whom Jesus loved" [John 20:2] affirmed that when he entered the empty tomb and discovered "the linen cloths lying there" [John 20:6], "he saw and believed." This suggests that he realized from the empty tomb's condition that the absence of Jesus' body could not have been of human doing and that Jesus had not simply returned to earthly life as had been the case with Lazarus.

Catechism of the Catholic Church 640

61

ẼDIT SVP CELOS ⁊VOLAVIT SVP PẼ ÑAS VENTORVM·PS·X

⁊ VÑVS POSTꝊLOCVTVS Ẽ ASSVͨTVS Ẽ ĪCELVM. M̃. VLTĪ·

Fra Angelico, *The Ascension of Christ* from the series of paintings on the Armadio degli Argenti (Silver Chest), tempera on wood, 38.5 x 37 cm, Florence, Museum of San Marco.

2. The Ascension

Fra Angelico, *The Ascension of Christ*

This painting is the work of Fra Angelico (1395–ca. 1455). It is painted in tempera on wood (1451–53), and housed in Florence at the Museum of San Marco. The artist wished to capture the moment immediately following the ascension. Jesus' body is gone, and is now wrapped in the glory of heaven. However, precisely because the body of Jesus is no longer visible to the human eye, the artist has chosen to represent the first Church gathered in prayer. Here, arranged in a circle as a sign of universality and unity, are Mary and the apostles kneeling on the ground and looking heavenward. When the physical body of Christ is no longer visible, the Body of the Church—the Body of Christ—comes into being. The angel on the right is turned toward the apostles, asking them why they are looking up in the sky, and announcing to them the second coming of Jesus.

So when they had come together, they asked him, "Lord, is this the time when you will restore the kingdom to Israel?" He replied, "It is not for you to know the times or periods that the Father has set by his own authority. But you will receive power when the Holy Spirit has come upon you; and you will be my witnesses in Jerusalem, in all Judea and Samaria, and to the ends of the earth." When he had said this, as they were watching, he was lifted up, and a cloud took him out of their sight. While he was going and they were gazing up toward heaven, suddenly two men in white robes stood by them. They said, "Men of Galilee, why do you stand looking up toward heaven? This Jesus, who has been taken up from you into heaven, will come in the same way as you saw him go into heaven."

Acts 1:6–11

Jesus, the Son of Man

The Jews were waiting for the Son of Man who would, as described in Daniel, descend from the clouds of heaven.

"As I watched in the night visions, I saw one like a human being coming with the clouds of heaven. And he came to the Ancient One and was presented before him. To him was given dominion and glory and kingship, that all peoples, nations, and languages should serve him. His dominion is an everlasting dominion that shall not pass away, and his kingship is one that shall never be destroyed" (Dan 7:13–14).

Elijah is the only example of ascension into heaven in the Old Testament. Elijah disappeared from Elisha's sight when a chariot and horses of fire passed between them. When the chariot disappeared, Elijah was gone.

Jesus' contemporaries confused him with Elijah because he performed similar miracles, but he was not Elijah.

After spending some time with the disciples, Jesus returns to the Father from whence he came; in other words, "he ascended into Heaven." This expression makes it clear that the risen Christ has gone back to God the Father in "heaven," that is, up where the ancients thought that God must be.

The Promise of the Holy Spirit

Just as the prophet Elijah had bequeathed his cloak to his disciple Elisha, in order that the apostles might continue the mission of their Master, Jesus leaves them the promise of an inheritance: Jesus wants his apostles to continue his mission, his work, and leaves the Twelve the promise that he will send them the Holy Spirit (Acts 2:1–4).

It will be the Holy Spirit who will help them and guide them, so that they can be authentic witnesses of his preaching and of the experiences he underwent in his passion, death, and resurrection.

Elijah had been taken up to heaven by God, but Jesus goes to the Father under his own power. Until the ascension of Jesus, the disciples, in accordance with Jewish tradition, would have thought that the heavens could be opened only in one direction, from God to men and not vice versa.

Jesus' ascension into heaven, however, does not affect only him; it is for humanity. Jesus goes to the Father and opens the heavens, which, from that moment onward, are no longer a place from which human beings are excluded.

The ascension of Jesus is also a model, an example offered to humankind so that we might understand where our destiny lies. Just as Jesus ascended to the Father, so the same will also happen to those who believe in him.

"So then the Lord Jesus, after he had spoken to them, was taken up into heaven, and sat down at the right hand of God" [Mark 16:19]. Christ's body was glorified at the moment of his Resurrection, as proved by the new and supernatural properties it subsequently and permanently enjoys. But during the forty days when he eats and drinks familiarly with his disciples and teaches them about the kingdom, his glory remains veiled under the appearance of ordinary humanity. Jesus' final apparition ends with the irreversible entry of his humanity into divine glory, symbolized by the cloud and by heaven, where he is seated from that time forward at God's right hand. Only in a wholly exceptional and unique way would Jesus show himself to Paul "as to one untimely born" [1 Cor 15:8], in a last apparition that established him as an apostle.

The veiled character of the glory of the Risen One during this time is intimated in his mysterious words to Mary Magdalene: "I have not yet ascended to the Father; but go to my brethren and say to them, I am ascending to my Father and your Father, to my God and your God" [John 20:17]. This indicates a difference in manifestation between the glory of the risen Christ and that of the Christ exalted to the Father's right hand, a transition marked by the historical and transcendent event of the Ascension.

Catechism of the Catholic Church 659–60

School of Richenau, **The Descent of the Holy Spirit**, miniature from a Gospel manuscript from the tenth to the eleventh centuries, Folio 39v, Brescia, Queriniana Library

3. The Descent of the Holy Spirit

School of Richenau,
The Descent of the Holy Spirit

The descent of the Spirit on the day of Pentecost has been rendered by artists following fairly rigid iconography: usually the Holy Spirit, in the form of tongues of fire, descends on the Virgin Mary and the apostles who are gathered together in the Upper Room. Occasionally, at the top and in the middle, a dove, representing the Spirit, seems to descend on the group of apostles and on Mary. The scheme by which these compositions are organized is similar to the one used for the Last Supper, which had also taken place in the Upper Room. In the Pentecost scene, Jesus is replaced by Mary, while Matthias replaces Judas. In this way, the unity of the apostles is reestablished. In this icon, we can see twelve men captured at the moment when the Holy Spirit descended upon them in the form of tongues of fire. It is Pentecost, the day of the "birth" of the Church founded by Jesus, which is composed of the twelve apostles who were sent by him to spread the message of salvation throughout the world, which is symbolized by the book that each of them holds in his hand. Everything exudes power, joy, and security. After so many days living in hiding and in fear, now the twelve are filled with courage, they are no longer afraid, they speak openly to the people, and they will bring the gospel to the four corners of the world.

On the day of Pentecost when the seven weeks of Easter had come to an end, Christ's Passover is fulfilled in the outpouring of the Holy Spirit, manifested, given, and communicated as a divine person: of his fullness, Christ, the Lord, pours out the Spirit in abundance.
On that day, the Holy Trinity is fully revealed. Since that day, the Kingdom announced by Christ has been open to those who believe in him: in the humility of the flesh and in faith, they already share in the communion of the Holy Trinity. By his coming, which never ceases, the Holy Spirit causes the world to enter into the "last days," the time of the Church, the Kingdom already inherited though not yet consummated.
Catechism of the Catholic Church 731–32

When the day of Pentecost had come, they were all together in one place. And suddenly from heaven there came a sound like the rush of a violent wind, and it filled the entire house where they were sitting. Divided tongues, as of fire, appeared among them, and a tongue rested on each of them. All of them were filled with the Holy Spirit and began to speak in other languages, as the Spirit gave them ability.

Now there were devout Jews from every nation under heaven living in Jerusalem. And at this sound the crowd gathered and was bewildered, because each one heard them speaking in the native language of each. Amazed and astonished, they asked, "Are not all these who are speaking Galileans? And how is it that we hear, each of us, in our own native language? Parthians, Medes, Elamites, and residents of Mesopotamia, Judea and Cappadocia, Pontus and Asia, Phrygia and Pamphylia, Egypt and the parts of Libya belonging to Cyrene, and visitors from Rome, both Jews and proselytes, Cretans and Arabs—in our own languages we hear them speaking about God's deeds of power." All were amazed and perplexed, saying to one another, "What does this mean?" But others sneered and said, "They are filled with new wine."

Acts 2:1–13

The Pentecost of the Spirit

The word *Pentecost* is of Greek origin and refers to the fifty days between the conclusion of Passover and the Feast of Weeks (Shavuot). Initially, it was a feast of thanksgiving for the harvest, but later it was enriched to commemorate God giving the Ten Commandments to Moses on Mount Sinai. Luke is interested in this second meaning. He connects the episode of the Upper Room with the giving of the Law to Moses on Sinai. In the Upper Room, all those who were praying received tongues of fire, which rested on their heads.

The descent of the Holy Spirit profoundly changes the people who receive it, instilling in them the strength to sustain their faith and the courage to decide to witness to the risen Christ.

Those who had gathered in the Upper Room believed that Jesus had risen from the dead, but it is one thing to know the truth with one's mind and quite another to have the courage to testify to it.

It is the Holy Spirit who opens the hearts of the apostles. The moment Jesus died on the cross, the veil of the temple was torn open and the Glory of God abandoned the temple. Now the Holy Spirit appears in the form of flame (like the burning bush on Sinai) and comes down permanently on the apostles. The heart then is the abode of the Holy Spirit. With the gift of the Spirit, the apostles receive the strength to be faithful to Jesus and to obey his request: "Go and preach baptizing them in the name of the Father, and of the Son and of the Holy Spirit."

The Courage of the Word

The words that come from the mouths of the apostles are understood by the crowd, even though they belong to the Jewish Diaspora, and therefore speak different languages. Reading these verses reminds us of the phenomenon of glossalalia or speaking in tongues, when the power of the Holy Spirit causes the speaker to use foreign words. It seems that in the communities that Paul founded this phenomenon was well known. However, its meaning goes even deeper. In the story of the Tower of Babel, the one language used by all human beings had been divided, while here we witness the reconstitution of humanity. Language, a cause of division and misunderstanding among humankind, is now the means of reaching a new unity that comes about through proclaiming the resurrection of Jesus that is brought to all humankind and is understandable to everyone. With the gift of the Spirit, the life of the first Christian community begins and the Church, the family of God's children, is born.

The Holy Spirit is the greatest protagonist in the Book of Acts. Invisible but always present, the Spirit advises, helps, and encourages the apostles, the disciples, and the believers so they may carry out their various missions. There are no important actions that the Church takes that are not implemented in accordance with the will and with the counsel of the Holy Spirit. He reveals himself to the apostles and to the community, especially at their communal meetings and during prayer.

Cola dell'Amatrice (Nicola Filotesio), *Assumption of the Virgin with Saints Lawrence, Benedict, Mary Magdalene and Scholastica*, 1516, painted on wood, altarpiece, central compartment 204 x 136.5 cm, side compartments 119 x 72 cm, Vatican City, Vatican Apostolic Palace, Vatican Picture Gallery, Room VII.

4. The Assumption

This work was executed by Nicola Filotesio, known as Cola dell'Amatrice (1480–1559).

The observer's eye is drawn to the group of apostles placed at the bottom of the painting, who are intent on examining the empty tomb of the Virgin. They are taken aback. Just as the women had found the empty tomb of Jesus, so the apostles can see that the body of the Virgin Mary is missing. The viewer's gaze follows the eyes of various characters who are in search of Mary's body, and is directed upward because one member of the group raises his face to look at the sky where he finds the Mother of God ascending; another figure stretches out his hands toward her. The artist depicts Mary standing on the clouds that hold her up; the higher the clouds rise, the more they take on a luminous quality. Mary's face and body are enveloped in light and surrounded by angels who are there to serve her. Mary's face is turned toward the apostles as she looks down on them from above as if to intercede for them and for all humanity.

And Mary said, "My soul magnifies the Lord, and my spirit rejoices in God my Savior, for he has looked with favor on the lowliness of his servant. Surely, from now on all generations will call me blessed; for the Mighty One has done great things for me, and holy is his name. His mercy is for those who fear him from generation to generation. He has shown strength with his arm; he has scattered the proud in the thoughts of their hearts. He has brought down the powerful from their thrones, and lifted up the lowly; he has filled the hungry with good things, and sent the rich away empty. He has helped his servant Israel, in remembrance of his mercy, according to the promise he made to our ancestors, to Abraham and to his descendants forever."

Luke 1:46–55

The Magnificat

The heartfelt song that bursts forth from Mary in response to Elizabeth's words reminds us of some passages in the Old Testament, including the song of Hannah in 1 Samuel 2:1–10. The main elements that we can find in these verses are the following:

–Mary thanks God for the favor he has granted to her;
–Mary remembers the special mercy of God to the poor, while he does not intervene in favor of the rich and powerful;
–Israel is always at the center of the love of God who intervenes in its history;
–Mary interprets what she is experiencing in the light of the history of all God's people.

Mary gives praise directly to God whom she identifies as Savior, the one who intervenes to defend Israel. Despite the greatness of God's plan for her, she considers herself nothing more than the Lord's servant. Regardless of this, and because of divine intervention, she will be recognized as blessed by all generations. There is a big difference between what Mary thinks of herself, her emptiness and lowliness, and what others recognize in her. Mary is humble, but her humility consists not in affirming that she is worth nothing, but in recognizing the immense gift that God has given her.

Mary, Daughter of Israel

Mary does not stand apart, but is fully integrated into God's people, and that is why she begins to present the history of Israel in the light of the saving interventions accomplished by God almost like a metaphor of the decisive intervention that the Lord has worked in her through the incarnation of his Son. It is precisely with the incarnation that God enters into humanity, visits his people, and takes a permanent dwelling among human beings (Exod 40:35; 2 Sam 6:9), a pure dwelling place, different than that of the temple in Jerusalem that was periodically defiled by pagans.

Again, Mary recalls the holiness of God's name. While once the sanctity of God's name was a source of terror for human beings (one who saw God would die, according to the ancients), here the power of God does not evoke fear, but arouses in Mary a recognition of his greatness, wonder at all that he has done, the joy of the merciful love that for centuries he has poured out on his people and that now he pours out again, becoming flesh and blood in his plan to share humanity's fate forever, in a spirit of trustworthy faithfulness.

The Wonders of God

As God acts throughout history, he demonstrates that he works with a different mindset from that of humanity. While humanity considers it most beneficial to intervene in favor of the rich and powerful, God proves himself the guarantor, the avenger, and the savior of the poor and needy. God's mercy on the poor was present in the Old Testament, but here the anawim, the poor of God, are exalted, and just as in the Beatitudes (Luke 6:20ff., which forms the center of Jesus' preaching) they will even be called blessed.

Between God and Israel a covenant had been established, and God is true to his word. What God promises, he does, and his word is always efficacious. Mary attests to the faithfulness of a God who cannot forget his people and who helps them.

The last act to complete his promises is the incarnation of his Son, the sending of a Messiah. God had promised a son to Abraham and an everlasting lineage of descendants to David (Gen 12:2; 2 Sam 7:13). Now God keeps those promises.

Mary, a Model for the Church

The Church believes that Mary rose bodily into heaven. However, her experience is quite different from that of Jesus. In fact, the Church teaches that the Virgin Mary was "assumed" into heaven by God; she did not go there under her own power.

Mary's assumption symbolizes the promise of the resurrection of the body for all believers, which will take place when Christ returns on the last day.

To understand this truth of faith it is worth recalling that the foundation of Christianity, the fundamental element that gives meaning to all is hope in the resurrection, the certainty that death, despite how things appear, does not have the last word. So Paul says, "But in fact Christ has been raised from the dead, the first fruits of those who have died" (1 Cor 15:20). By his resurrection, Jesus opened the way and is waiting for all who believe in him. Mary's assumption reminds us that what happened to Jesus is not restricted to the God-made-man. Just as Jesus rose from the dead, so everyone who unites him- or herself to his passion and death will one day rise again. Mary is believed by the Church to be the one in whom the realization of what awaits every human being is anticipated and in this she is also our model.

Mary is now beyond death; she has overcome the barrier that awaits every person and lives in "heaven." So we can say that Mary is the first fruits of those who rise from the dead and the image of the Church. However, we need to clarify that Mary's assumption is the culmination of what began when the Virgin gave her yes to God. For Christians, eternal life is not something detached from this life but begins here on earth and is measured by our ability to love. Only love is able to give an account of our faith and of the hope that is in us. It is thanks to the love that fills Mary that the Virgin is able to burst forth singing the Magnificat, but is also able to express even further her openness to the hope in what God will do in the future, an openness to what does not yet exist, but that will be realized only in the kingdom of God. It is only in that dimension that those who are hungry will be truly satisfied and that the poor will ultimately find justice. Mary acknowledges that she is loved by God, and it is in experiencing this love first that she finds the ability to love others.

It is in Mary that love, God who is Love, was made flesh, and this has allowed Mary to enter into and let all of humanity enter into what had long been considered the place that was exclusive to God: heaven.

"Finally the Immaculate Virgin, preserved free from all stain of original sin, when the course of her earthly life was finished, was taken up body and soul into heavenly glory, and exalted by the Lord as Queen over all things, so that she might be the more fully conformed to her Son, the Lord of lords and conqueror of sin and death." The Assumption of the Blessed Virgin is a singular participation in her Son's Resurrection and an anticipation of the resurrection of other Christians.

Catechism of the Catholic Church 966

Bernardino di Betto (Pintoricchio), ***Coronation of the Virgin***, 1503, tempera on wood panel, transferred to canvas, 330 x 200 cm, Vatican City, Vatican Apostolic Palaces, Vatican Picture Gallery, Room VII.

5. *The Coronation*

This painting was executed by Bernardino di Betto, known as Pinturicchio (Perugia, 1454–Siena, 1513). It is a tempera painting on wood dating from 1503.

In the upper part of the painting, the artist wanted to portray the coronation of the Virgin. Christ and Mary are included in a beautiful, almond-shaped halo of divine light, surrounded by a chorus of angels. To the right and left the artist has placed two musical angels.

In the lower part of the work are portraits of Saints Francis of Assisi, Bernardine of Siena, Anthony of Padua, Ludwig of Toulouse, and Bonaventure among the twelve apostles, as if to emphasize their importance in giving testimony to the faith.

In the scene, Jesus is crowning his Mother, placing on her head a very beautiful crown. Mary keeps her hands clasped in prayer and her head slightly bowed, showing the humility, even at the moment of her glorification, that had set her apart from the moment of the annunciation, when she was recognized as the humble servant of the Lord. Here the humble servant receives the honors of both heaven and earth.

Then God's temple in heaven was opened, and the ark of his covenant was seen within his temple; and there were flashes of lightning, rumblings, peals of thunder, an earthquake, and heavy hail.

A great portent appeared in heaven: a woman clothed with the sun, with the moon under her feet, and on her head a crown of twelve stars. She was pregnant and was crying out in birth pangs, in the agony of giving birth. Then another portent appeared in heaven: a great red dragon, with seven heads and ten horns, and seven diadems on his heads. His tail swept down a third of the stars of heaven and threw them to the earth. Then the dragon stood before the woman who was about to bear a child, so that he might devour her child as soon as it was born. And she gave birth to a son, a male child, who is to rule all the nations with a rod of iron. But her child was snatched away and taken to God and to his throne; and the woman fled into the wilderness, where she has a place prepared by God, so that there she can be nourished for one thousand two hundred sixty days. And war broke out in heaven; Michael and his angels fought against the dragon. The dragon and his angels fought back, but they were defeated, and there was no longer any place for them in heaven. The great dragon was thrown down, that ancient serpent, who is called the Devil and Satan, the deceiver of the whole world—he was thrown down to the earth, and his angels were thrown down with him. Then I heard a loud voice in heaven, proclaiming, "Now have come the salvation and the power and the kingdom of our God and the authority of his Messiah, for the accuser of our comrades has been thrown down, who accuses them day and night before our God."

Revelation 11:19—12:10

The Heavenly Jerusalem and the Woman

This passage begins with a description of the temple of God in heaven. The temple in Jerusalem, which had long been the only legitimate sanctuary for worshipping God, is now gone, destroyed by the Romans. Since then, Christians have understood that we can worship God in any place.

The presence of the ark of the covenant indicates the presence of God among his people. The description that follows is a fulfillment of the promises that appear in Genesis 3:15-16. In the vision, a woman represents the Jewish people as well as the Church, and Mary, the new Eve, should be understood as the true daughter of Zion. The woman gives birth to the Messiah in great pain while an enemy appears, a huge dragon that is the symbol of evil and of all that is against God and his people who are in covenant with him, and of Satan (the accuser, Zech 3:1-2; Job 1:6). The dragon would have devoured the child, but he is caught up by God, a sign of the triumph of Christ. The woman flees into the wilderness, which in the Bible is an in-between place, a place of solitude and temptation, yet also a place where God is revealed. Here the just of the Old Testament can find shelter when they are persecuted (Exod 2:15; 1 Kgs 19:3ff.; 1 Macc 2:29-30). Here the woman remains for three and a half years, which is a way of indicating the persecution.

The birth of the Messiah unleashes the final struggle between good and evil, between the children of light and children of darkness, between Satan and his hosts and Michael (which means "Who is like God?") and his angels. It is a colossal struggle, but the forces of evil will not prevail.

The Church, Bride of Christ

It is interesting to call to mind a short passage in Isaiah, referring to Israel, that says, "You shall be a crown of beauty in the hand of the Lord... but you shall be called My Delight Is in Her, and your land Married; for the Lord delights in you" (Isa 62:3, 4). Israel is the nation that God loved with a love that transcends the boundaries of time (Jer 31:1). Loved by God forever and always, Israel has been married by God "in righteousness and in justice, in steadfast love, and in mercy" (Hos 2:19). For the author of Revelation, the Church is the bride of the Lamb (Rev 21:9). Just as Israel is loved by God, Christ loves the Church to the point that he "gave himself up for her, in order to make her holy" (Eph 5:25–26). Here in the vision, a woman appears crowned with twelve stars, one star for each tribe of Israel.

Mary's Crown

The crown that Mary wears is not her own. As we can see from the iconography, Mary is crowned by the Son. It is Jesus who, "crowned with glory and honor" (Heb 2:9) himself, is able to crown Mary. We can understand this detail well if we observe carefully the elements included in the passage. Mary is surrounded by stars and under her feet there is the moon, but as the moon shines by the light of the sun, so Mary shines by the light of Christ. Mary, who has been assumed into heaven, is already in the sanctuary where Jesus has gone as the first fruits of humanity. The Virgin, preserved from original sin in view of the incarnation of Christ, lived the fullness of human life by exercising virtue.

"All generations will call me blessed": "The Church's devotion to the Blessed Virgin is intrinsic to Christian worship." The Church rightly honors "the Blessed Virgin with special devotion. From the most ancient times the Blessed Virgin has been honored with the title of 'Mother of God,' to whose protection the faithful fly in all their dangers and needs....This very special devotion...differs essentially from the adoration which is given to the incarnate Word and equally to the Father and the Holy Spirit, and greatly fosters this adoration." The liturgical feasts dedicated to the Mother of God and Marian prayer, such as the rosary, an "epitome of the whole Gospel," express this devotion to the Virgin Mary.

Catechism of the Catholic Church 971

The Luminous Mysteries

Piero della Francesca, ***The Baptism of Christ***, 1440–ca.1460, tempera on wood, 167 x 116 cm, London, National Gallery.

1. The Baptism in the Jordan

> Piero della Francesca, *The Baptism of Christ*

Jesus, who is being baptized by John the Baptist, occupies the central area of this painting. In the sky, you see the dove, the symbol of the Holy Spirit. On the left, we see three angels, and on the right is a figure who is undressing in preparation for baptism. In the background are characters who appear to be priests: one of them is pointing to the sky. The gesture of this priest seems to copy that of John the Baptist who raises above Jesus' head the water container with which he will baptize Jesus. The village in the background represents Jerusalem. If we examine this work by Piero della Francesca, we can pick out some interesting details:

–The work is constructed by placing a circle above a square. The Holy Spirit is in the exact center of the circle and its wings are open across the diameter; the center of the square is positioned on the navel of Christ, which becomes its most important point;

–If we draw a line starting from the Holy Spirit and trace it toward the bottom, we find the container with water and the hand of John, Jesus' head, and Jesus' hands joined in prayer. Our gaze then stops at the feet of Jesus, which are in the water, the lowest point of the composition. The central elements of the composition are all grouped around this axis;

–There is a geometric and chromatic parallel between the tree and Christ;

–None of the characters has a halo on his head;

–The course of the river Jordan stops at the feet of Jesus.

According to some commentators, the nut tree in the foreground is a symbol of the tree of the cross; according to others the nut tree, which is favored for its fruit, is linked to symbolism according to which the husk represents human nature, the kernel divine nature, and the shell the wood of the cross.

In those days Jesus came from Nazareth of Galilee and was baptized by John in the Jordan. And just as he was coming up out of the water, he saw the heavens torn apart and the Spirit descending like a dove on him. And a voice came from heaven, "You are my Son, the Beloved; with you I am well pleased."

Mark 1:9–11

Jesus' Commitment to Do the Will of the Father

The Synoptic Gospels tell us that Jesus was baptized by John the Baptist. This baptism required of those who wished to be baptized repentance, conversion, and a commitment to change their way of life.

However, one fact is important to understand: we cannot maintain that Jesus had sinned; he had nothing to repent of or be converted from. However, this does not make his baptism invalid. Jesus' baptism gave witness that he adhered to the Father's will.

What happens to Jesus is more reminiscent of the anointing of the kings of Israel. While other kings could show a crown to indicate their royalty, the kings of Israel could boast an anointing. On the head of the king was poured scented and consecrated oil, contained in a ram's horn (1 Sam 16:13; Judg 3:10). Jesus receives the Spirit and is thus anointed King of God's people. Anointed with oil, Jesus is the Messiah, or in Greek, Christ.

The Israelites were waiting for a Messiah, a man of God, a Savior who would deliver them from slavery. Throughout history, different types of Messiah were awaited: king, priest, prophet. The Church, the New and Eternal Israel, instead has recognized all three of these types in Jesus' role as Messiah.

God Breaks into History and Reveals the Son

The heavens "are opened," according to an expression often used in literature that is as prophetic as it is apocalyptic (Isa 63:19; Ezek 1:1; John 1:51; Acts 7:51; 10:1; Rev 10:11); it is an image that refers to the irruption of divinity into humanity's history. The God of Israel, as the Old

Testament presents him, does not remain aloof, but actively intervenes in human history. However, the scope of the message goes beyond this understanding. In fact, Jesus became incarnate in humanity; Jesus is God and man. The heavens are always broken open, in him and for him. In this close relationship with his Father, Jesus hears the words, "You are my Son, the Beloved; with you I am well pleased," words that remind us of Psalm 2:7, a royal psalm in which God publicly declares before the assembly of Israel his intention to adopt the king, a descendent of David, as his own son (2 Sam 7:14). The New Testament has interpreted these Old Testament passages as referring directly to Jesus Christ, the true King because he is the true Son of God.

God is pleased with the Son because Jesus is loved in a special way by the Father who delights in everything he does, and each offering is pleasing to him.

So we witness a royal election, but also a prophetic anointing similar to that described by Isaiah (6). Through his baptism, Jesus begins his mission of proclamation and salvation.

Jesus' messianic consecration reveals his divine mission, "for the name 'Christ' implies 'he who anointed,' 'he who was anointed' and 'the very anointing with which he was anointed.' The one who anointed is the Father, the one who was anointed is the Son, and he was anointed with the Spirit who is the anointing." His eternal messianic consecration was revealed during the time of his earthly life at the moment of his baptism by John, when "God anointed Jesus of Nazareth with the Holy Spirit and with power," "that he might be revealed to Israel" as its Messiah. His works and words will manifest him as "the Holy One of God."

Catechism of the Catholic Church 438

2. The Wedding at Cana

The image here is a painting by Hieronymus Bosch in oil on board, executed in 1616 and housed in the Boijmans Van Beuningen Museum in Rotterdam.

The artist has set the first of Jesus' miracles described in the Gospel of John in a room decorated as befits a wedding. One of the elements that immediately strikes the viewer is that this first sign of Jesus takes place amid the indifference of the diners, who are intent on carousing.

The figure who appears in the background dressed in white with a rod in his hand is probably an innkeeper. To the left, servants are bringing two trays to the table on which are set a boar's head and a swan, both piping hot.

At the center, in front of the table but facing the back, you can see the figure of a cupbearer wearing a white sash. The bride and bridegroom are also at the center of the scene. Jesus is placed to the right and his right hand is raised in a gesture of blessing.

Down at the bottom a servant is pouring water into wine pitchers that are placed in a prominent place and that alone indicates what the meaning of the composition is.

Hieronymus Bosch (attributed, **The Marriage Feast at Cana**, 1516, oil on board, 93 x 72 cm, Rotterdam, Boijmans Van Beuningen Museum.

On the third day there was a wedding in Cana of Galilee, and the mother of Jesus was there. Jesus and his disciples had also been invited to the wedding. When the wine gave out, the mother of Jesus said to him, "They have no wine." And Jesus said to her, "Woman, what concern is that to you and to me? My hour has not yet come." His mother said to the servants, "Do whatever he tells you." Now standing there were six stone water jars for the Jewish rites of purification, each holding twenty or thirty gallons. Jesus said to them, "Fill the jars with water." And they filled them up to the brim. He said to them, "Now draw some out, and take it to the chief steward." So they took it. When the steward tasted the water that had become wine, and did not know where it came from (though the servants who had drawn the water knew), the steward called the bridegroom and said to him, "Everyone serves the good wine first, and then the inferior wine after the guests have become drunk. But you have kept the good wine until now." Jesus did this, the first of his signs, in Cana of Galilee, and revealed his glory; and his disciples believed in him.

John 2:1–11

The First of the "Signs"

This is the first of Jesus' signs recorded in the Gospel of John. Jesus begins to manifest himself during a wedding feast. This image recurs in the texts of the prophets and in the poetry of the Song of Songs, one of those images that the biblical writers use to indicate the special relationship between God and his people. Israel is the bride of YHWH, who loves her very much, so much that he is jealous for her.

Jesus and his mother Mary are invited to this wedding feast, and Mary becomes aware of a difficult situation for the newlyweds: they have no more wine. Mary is present for this miracle and was present under the cross (John 10:25–27). The presence of Mary is a clue that the two scenes are linked together. Wedding feasts in the East could last as much as a week and generally the whole village participated. It was also customary to bring some wine as a gift for the newlyweds, just to meet their needs.

Jesus calls Mary "woman," a special way of a son addressing his mother. Beneath the cross Mary will also be called "woman." Mary is the "woman," the mother of all humanity. Jesus wants to emphasize that his hour has not yet come and that therefore any sign he performed would be out of place.

Jesus' Hour

For John the hour is not just any time, but it is the moment when Jesus will be glorified on the cross. The Father has set this hour and it cannot be anticipated by anyone else. The death on the cross is indeed the moment of utmost annihilation, but also of utmost glorification. For John, it is from the cross that Jesus communicated the Holy Spirit to humanity because, when the centurion struck the side of Jesus, blood and water came out from the wound. This water is a sign of the Spirit being communicated to humanity. Jesus' hour in this episode of the wedding can also be understood as the time when the Master begins to show visible signs that will be accepted by some people, while others, those who do not know how to interpret them, reject them. Jesus turns water into wine and by this sign anticipates his death and resurrection.

The sign of water turned into wine at Cana already announces the Hour of Jesus' glorification. It makes manifest the fulfillment of the wedding feast in the Father's kingdom, where the faithful will drink the new wine that has become the Blood of Christ.

Catechism of the Catholic Church 1335

James Tissot, *Christ Teaches in the Synagogue*, ca. 1894, watercolor, 26.8 x 19.2 cm, London, Bridgeman Art Library.

3. The Proclamation of the Kingdom of God

James Tissot,
Christ Teaches in the Synagogue

This work is a watercolor belonging to the series "The Life of Our Lord Jesus Christ" by James Tissot, which was painted circa 1894. Today it is housed at the Bridgeman Art Library in London.

The artist has portrayed Jesus in the center of the scene while he reads from the scroll of Isaiah. Look carefully at the elements that the artist captures in fine detail so that the viewer almost has the impression of being present at the scene. The figure next to Jesus wears a *tallit* or prayer shawl, covering his head and shoulders. Jesus is reading from the scroll. On the scroll can be seen the wooden rods that are used to roll up the sacred text. The covering for the Scriptures is richly worked. The artist almost "photographed" the event, as described in Luke 4:16 and following, where Jesus takes the scroll and reads the prophecy of Isaiah and then he offers his comment, whereby the Nazarene forces his countrymen to take sides for or against him.

When he came to Nazareth, where he had been brought up, he went to the synagogue on the sabbath day, as was his custom. He stood up to read, and the scroll of the prophet Isaiah was given to him. He unrolled the scroll and found the place where it was written: "The Spirit of the Lord is upon me, because he has anointed me to bring good news to the poor. He has sent me to proclaim release to the captives and recovery of sight to the blind, to let the oppressed go free, to proclaim the year of the Lord's favor." And he rolled up the scroll, gave it back to the attendant, and sat down. The eyes of all in the synagogue were fixed on him. Then he began to say to them, "Today this scripture has been fulfilled in your hearing." All spoke well of him and were amazed at the gracious words that came from his mouth. They said, "Is not this Joseph's son?" He said to them, "Doubtless you will quote to me this proverb, 'Doctor, cure yourself!' And you will say, 'Do here also in your hometown the things that we have heard you did at Capernaum.'" And he said, "Truly I tell you, no prophet is accepted in the prophet's hometown. But the truth is, there were many widows in Israel in the time of Elijah, when the heaven was shut up three years and six months, and there was a severe famine over all the land; yet Elijah was sent to none of them except to a widow at Zarephath in Sidon. There were also many lepers in Israel in the time of the prophet Elisha, and none of them was cleansed except Naaman the Syrian." When they heard this, all in the synagogue were filled with rage. They got up, drove him out of the town, and led him to the brow of the hill on which their town was built, so that they might hurl him off the cliff. But he passed through the midst of them and went on his way.

Luke 4:16–30

Jesus the Good Israelite

Every adult male Jew has the opportunity to read the Scriptures in the liturgy of the synagogue. As Jesus reads a passage from the Prophet Isaiah (Isa 61:1-2), he presents himself as the long-awaited Messiah who was to give liberty to the slaves and release to the prisoners. The passage speaks of giving freedom and sight, but also grace, the grace that comes from the year of the Lord's favor, the time when God forgives all who come to him with a contrite, poor, and humble heart. This is when the peace of God is established, because the time is ripe. It is therefore an announcement of liberation.

Jesus Reveals Himself

By reading these few verses, Jesus came before the inhabitants of Nazareth very clearly, unequivocally stating his message. The core of this message appears here, at the beginning of his preaching, but will be taken up again, developed, and will become more detailed through the rest of the Gospel. Shocking his hearers, Jesus claims that what was proclaimed about the Messiah was taking place right at that moment in time.

Division Because of Jesus

These words raise two different reactions in those who heard them: some listeners are aware that Jesus is speaking with authority; others cannot accept what Jesus is saying because he does not meet their expectations. They thought the Messiah was supposed to manifest himself suddenly and no one would know his relatives. But in Nazareth, all know Jesus as the son of Mary and of the carpenter Joseph. Furthermore, Jesus is a character who does not exhibit the characteristics of a powerful leader, who would be able to bring victory against the Romans. He is not rich, and therefore he cannot feed them as the awaited Messiah would have done. Being the son of a carpenter, he is not even a priest. In short, they expected someone much more striking than he is. Jesus, however, speaks with authority, but this very attitude suggests to his fellow citizens that he is out of his mind, and that he is a braggart.

Although he is accepted by many who followed him when he was teaching in their synagogues (Luke 4:14–15), in this episode Jesus is rejected by those who expect him to perform the miracles in Nazareth that he did in Capernaum. In other words, even though they do not believe in him, they would still like Jesus to entertain them with his signs. They are seized more by curiosity about his unusual abilities than by the desire to see the saving action of God. The people of Nazareth behave exactly as their predecessors did against the prophets: they are unable to accept the words of Jesus and intend to kill him. However, they cannot hurt Jesus because it is not yet time for him to die.

"Now after John was arrested, Jesus came into Galilee, preaching the gospel of God, and saying: 'The time is fulfilled, and the kingdom of God is at hand: repent, and believe in the gospel'" [Mark 1:14–15]. "To carry out the will of the Father Christ inaugurated the kingdom of heaven on earth." Now the Father's will is "to raise up men to share in his own divine life." He does this by gathering men around his Son Jesus Christ. This gathering is the Church, "on earth the seed and beginning of that kingdom."

Christ stands at the heart of this gathering of men into the "family of God." By his word, through signs that manifest the reign of God, and by sending out his disciples, Jesus calls all people to come together around him. But above all in the great Paschal mystery—his death on the cross and his Resurrection—he would accomplish the coming of his kingdom. "And I, when I am lifted up from the earth, will draw all men to myself" [John 12:32]. Into this union with Christ all men are called.

Everyone is called to enter the kingdom. First announced to the children of Israel, this messianic kingdom is intended to accept men of all nations. To enter it, one must first accept Jesus' word....

The kingdom belongs to the poor and lowly, which means those who have accepted it with humble hearts. Jesus is sent to "preach good news to the poor" [Luke 14:18]; he declares them blessed, for "theirs is the kingdom of heaven" [Matt 5:3]. To them—the "little ones" the Father is pleased to reveal what remains hidden from the wise and the learned. Jesus shares the life of the poor, from the cradle to the cross; he experiences hunger, thirst and privation. Jesus identifies himself with the poor of every kind and makes active love toward them the condition for entering his kingdom.

Catechism of the Catholic Church 541–44

Raphael Sanzio and Giulio Romano, *The Transfiguration*, 1518–20, oil on wood, 405 x 278 cm, Vatican City, Apostolic Palace, Vatican Museums.

4. The Transfiguration

Raphael Sanzio and Giulio Romano,
The Transfiguration

As we look at this painting, we immediately realize that here Raphael wanted to include two illustrated scenes from the Gospel. In the lower part we can see the episode of the possessed man whom the apostles could not help. But the upper part is dominated by the luminous image of Christ who is transfigured and manifesting his divinity.

The lower part is as dark as the upper part is bright. The lower part is inhabited by evil represented by the demoniac, while the top is bright because Jesus, who is God, is there, and his human nature is luminous because it has not been wounded by evil. At the point in time when Jesus is transfigured, the body of the possessed man seems to have been thrown into a fit, as though the evil in him had been cured by the light of the transfigured Christ.

It is interesting to note how the light strikes the figure of Christ. In the transfiguration, Jesus shows his divinity. Yet the light, which does not shine on him but emanates from him, shines out on those who are watching the scene.

Jesus is not illuminated: Jesus is the light itself that comes into the world and is therefore able to give light to humankind, to illuminate the darkness that surrounds them, caused by sin that also gives rise to their ignorance. Jesus is talking with Moses and Elijah, who are lit by the same light of Christ, which even illuminates the Scriptures (the Law and the Prophets) that these two figures represent. Jesus has his arms outstretched in a way that dramatically joins his passion and death on the cross with his resurrection. Indeed, Raphael painted Christ as risen and it is the glory of the risen Christ that is spread.

The three apostles down at the bottom, on the summit of Mount Tabor, are overcome by fear, before this manifestation of the divinity of Jesus.

Now about eight days after these sayings Jesus took with him Peter and John and James, and went up on the mountain to pray. And while he was praying, the appearance of his face changed, and his clothes became dazzling white. Suddenly they saw two men, Moses and Elijah, talking to him. They appeared in glory and were speaking of his departure, which he was about to accomplish at Jerusalem. Now Peter and his companions were weighed down with sleep; but since they had stayed awake, they saw his glory and the two men who stood with him. Just as they were leaving him, Peter said to Jesus, "Master, it is good for us to be here; let us make three dwellings, one for you, one for Moses, and one for Elijah"— not knowing what he said. While he was saying this, a cloud came and overshadowed them; and they were terrified as they entered the cloud. Then from the cloud came a voice that said, "This is my Son, my Chosen; listen to him!" When the voice had spoken, Jesus was found alone. And they kept silent and in those days told no one any of the things they had seen.

Luke 9:28–36

Encountering God

For all ancient peoples meeting God was an extremely dangerous experience: to meet God face-to-face could mean being killed, because the deity is too big and powerful and thus able to crush a human being. And that is why the God of the Bible meets humans through intermediaries such as prophets and angels or communicates through dreams. Scripture testifies that only a few people had met God up close (the patriarchs, Moses). Only Moses is said to have seen God "face-to-face," which we can understand as the particular closeness of that prophet with the deity.

In this passage, we see Jesus, who reveals himself to Peter, James, and John, in the fullness of his divinity and in the glory of the Son of God, by which he anticipates what will happen after his death in Jerusalem, namely, his resurrection and ascension. They climb a mountain, just as

Moses had gone up to Sinai, where YHWH had manifested his glory (Exod 13:20f.; 33:9f.; 34:29).

While Jesus is praying his appearance changes, he is transfigured, and he allows those with him to perceive who he really is. A sign of the divinity of Jesus are his clothes, which become white and dazzling. At this point, two men appear, Moses and Elijah, who are the reference points for much of the bible; they also remind us of the two messengers that the women meet at Jesus' tomb, which lies open and empty.

Jesus is enveloped in the glory of God as was predicted by Daniel (Dan 7:13). Peter wants to build three tents or three huts, a reminder of Israel's time wandering in the wilderness. But while the apostle is speaking, a cloud surrounds them, which again is a sign of God's presence (as it was in Exodus) and envelops them all, causing the apostles to fear what is happening to them. In fact, they understand that God is manifesting himself.

From the cloud comes a voice that proclaims Jesus as the Son of God. However, he is destined to be ignored. That is why God asks those present to listen to him.

Peter, James, and John are heavy with sleep, a sleepiness that reminds us of what will take place in Gethsemane (Luke 22:45).

For a moment Jesus discloses his divine glory, confirming Peter's confession. He also reveals that he will have to go by the way of the cross at Jerusalem in order to "enter into his glory" [Luke 24:26]. Moses and Elijah had seen God's glory on the Mountain; the Law and the Prophets had announced the Messiah's sufferings. Christ's Passion is the will of the Father: the Son acts as God's servant; the cloud indicates the presence of the Holy Spirit.

Catechism of the Catholic Church 555

5. *The Institution of the Eucharist*

Cosimo Rosselli, *The Last Supper*

This painting is a fresco by Cosimo Rosselli, painted in 1481–82 for the Sistine Chapel.

The artist has arranged Jesus and the apostles around a large table in the shape of a horseshoe. All the characters are sitting on a bench similar to that used by monks. Only Judas is isolated and is positioned so that the viewer is looking at his back.

From the left we have James the Less, Philip, James the Greater, Andrew, Peter, Jesus, John, Bartholomew, Matthew, Thomas, Simon the Zealot, and Thaddeus.

In the background we can see a scene of Jesus' prayer in the Garden of Gethsemane.

Leonardo da Vinci, *The Last Supper*

This painting depicts the Last Supper, a fresco done in oil tempera on plaster by Leonardo da Vinci. For this painting he experimented with a new technique, but unfortunately, the condition of the site has prevented the fresco from being preserved perfectly.

The work is dated by scholars between 1494 and 1498, and it can be admired in the former refectory of the convent of Santa Mary delle Grazie in Milan, where Ludovico il Moro commissioned Leonardo to paint the fresco.

The setting for the painting is based on the passage in John 13:21–26, when Jesus announces to the apostles that one of them is just about to betray him. This is also confirmed by the absence of the cup of wine on the table.

Cosimo Rosselli and Biagio D'Antonio, *The Last Supper*, 1481–82, fresco, 349 x 570 cm, Vatican City, Vatican Apostolic Palace, the Sistine Chapel, north wall.

Leonardo da Vinci, *The Last Supper*, 1494–98, oil tempera on plaster, 460 x 880 cm, Milan, Refectory of Santa Maria delle Grazie.

Leonardo illustrates with his masterful brushstrokes the essential character of each of the figures, capturing them in the moment that it dawns on them with horror that one of them would betray Jesus. We must remember that this is not just a convivial scene, a situation in which people's feelings emerge normally, but it is Jesus' Last Supper, as described in the Gospels.

Leonardo had the idea of exploiting the topography of the refectory so that it appeared to extend onto the wall on which he was painting the fresco. Anyone observing this work has the feeling that the hall continues into the painting. The perspective used by the artist is outstanding. The light comes from two sources: the windows in the background and a window that simulates real light, which would have come from the window on the left that corresponded to a window that actually existed.

In the foreground, Leonardo places the table around which the diners are positioned. At the center is Jesus, a little isolated from the others. From his facial expression, with his mouth half open, we can surmise that he has just finished communicating the news to his companions. His head is slightly bowed, as if he were resigned. Jesus is also the dividing point between the two groups of apostles, those on the right and those on the left, each of which are then further divided into groups of three. Jesus, who is at the center of the whole composition, is also the only character who is still, because the groups of the apostles seem to be moved as though with a wave of fear and indignation, which starts from the center of the fresco and dies away a little toward the edges.

Even John, who is on Jesus' right (left from the viewer's point of view), recoils and speaks with Judas, who is clutching the bag of money. Peter holds a knife, thus showing part of his violent nature. Peter is leaning toward John, perhaps hoping to learn from him the name of the traitor (John 13:24). To the right of the table we find Matthew, Thaddeus, and Simon, who are incredulous and seem lost. James the Greater stands with his arms wide open like someone who can make no sense of it all. Philip, for his part, puts his hands to his chest and swears that he is not the one who is planning such a terrible deed. Thomas is immediately to the left of Jesus and has his finger pointing upward.

Then came the day of Unleavened Bread, on which the Passover lamb had to be sacrificed. So Jesus sent Peter and John, saying, "Go and prepare the Passover meal for us that we may eat it." They asked him, "Where do you want us to make preparations for it?" "Listen," he said to them, "when you have entered the city, a man carrying a jar of water will meet you; follow him into the house he enters and say to the owner of the house, 'The teacher asks you, "Where is the guest room, where I may eat the Passover with my disciples?"' He will show you a large room upstairs, already furnished. Make preparations for us there." So they went and found everything as he had told them; and they prepared the Passover meal. When the hour came, he took his place at the table, and the apostles with him. He said to them, "I have eagerly desired to eat this Passover with you before I suffer; for I tell you, I will not eat it until it is fulfilled in the kingdom of God." Then he took a cup, and after giving thanks he said, "Take this and divide it among yourselves; for I tell you that from now on I will not drink of the fruit of the vine until the kingdom of God comes." Then he took a loaf of bread, and when he had given thanks, he broke it and gave it to them, saying, "This is my body, which is given for you. Do this in remembrance of me." And he did the same with the cup after supper, saying, "This cup that is poured out for you is the new covenant in my blood."

Luke 22:7–20

Celebrating the Feast

During the week in which the whole community of Israel celebrates the great feast of the Passover, Jesus completes his mission and reaches the end of his earthly life.

In those days, Jesus celebrated the feast of the Passover with his friends: it is Jesus' Last Supper, which comes a few hours before his arrest, passion, and death.

During the Passover meal, the Israelites thank God for the wonders he has done over the centuries for their salvation. They recall the night of the Exodus and their liberation from slavery in Egypt.

With his extraordinary deeds, Jesus teaches that it is right to thank God for the salvation that he himself, the Risen One, has brought to humanity, freeing them from the slavery of sin and death.

Jesus eats his last Passover meal in an upper room (dining room) that was rented for the occasion. The feast of Passover is a family feast, but it was permitted for groups of disciples to gather to eat the Passover.

This is a time of intense intimacy between Jesus and his disciples, since eating and being together to celebrate naturally unites people. At two particular points in the celebration, the blessing of the unleavened bread and the blessing of the last chalice of wine, Jesus introduces a new element into the proceedings.

The Consecration of the Bread and Wine

After having blessed the unleavened bread, Jesus refers to the bread as his body, and after blessing the wine, he refers to the wine as his blood. The Passover bread then is a sign of Christ's body, while the Passover wine is a sign of Christ's blood.

At Passover, the Israelites sacrificed a lamb, which was then consumed during the dinner. Jesus compares himself to that lamb, slain and sacrificed for Passover. Just as the Israelites, until then, had fed from the flesh of the lamb and from the unleavened bread, so, from that moment on, every time the apostles remembered the covenant with YHWH, they would also eat the body of Christ. And so, just as formerly the Israelites had offered the blood of the lamb and drank the fruit of the vine, from then on they would drink the blood of Christ. The blood and the body begin a new and eternal covenant that will never fail.

In the past, a lamb was offered to establish or remember a covenant: Jesus offered himself and made it known that he is the new lamb of the new covenant. For the Israelites, the feast of the Passover is a memorial, a special liturgical time, in which is celebrated in the here and now something that happened in the past, but that actually becomes present.

For Catholics, the bread and wine of the Eucharist truly are the body and blood of Jesus Christ who is present in the Church that he founded. When the Church celebrates the Eucharist, Jesus is truly present.

Jesus gave the supreme expression of his free offering of himself at the meal shared with the twelve Apostles "on the night he was betrayed" [1 Cor 11:23]. On the eve of his Passion, while still free, Jesus transformed this Last Supper with the apostles into the memorial of his voluntary offering to the Father for the salvation of men: "This is my body which is given for you" [Luke 22:19.] "This is my blood of the covenant, which is poured out for many for the forgiveness of sins" [Matt 26:28].

The Eucharist that Christ institutes at that moment will be the memorial of his sacrifice. Jesus includes the apostles in his own offering and bids them perpetuate it. By doing so, the Lord institutes his apostles as priests of the New Covenant: "For their sakes I sanctify myself, so that they also may be sanctified in truth" [John 17:19].

Catechism of the Catholic Church 610–11

At the heart of the Eucharistic celebration are the bread and wine that, by the words of Christ and the invocation of the Holy Spirit, become Christ's Body and Blood. Faithful to the Lord's command the Church continues to do, in his memory and until his glorious return, what he did on the eve of his Passion: "He took bread…." "He took the cup filled with wine…."

Catechism of the Catholic Church 1333

Acknowledgments

Special thanks to the management of the Vatican Museums for kindly granting the use of the images from the Archives of the Museums and to the archives manager for the excellent work.

Image credits

© A. Dagli Orti / Scala Picture Library, Florence p. 66. © De Agostini Picture Library / Scala Picture Library, Florence p. 40, p. 42. © Photos from the Vatican Museums p. 1, p. 7, p. 13, p. 20, p. 31, p. 32, p. 45, p. 48, p. 56, p. 62, p. 70, p. 76, p. 81, p. 96, p. 101, top. © Photos from Ann Ronan / Heritage Images / Scala, Florence p. 90, p. 94. © Photos from Scala Picture Library, Florence p. 2, p. 8, p. 11, p. 55, p. 82. © Photos from Scala Picture Library, Florence / places of worship-the Ministry of the Interior p. 36, p. 39. © Photos from Scala Picture Library, Florence concession by the Ministry of Heritage and Cultural Activities p. 101, bottom. © Thyssen-Bornemisza Museum / Scala Picture Library, Florence p. 26. © Boijmans Van Beuningen Museum, Rotterdam p. 87.